PACKING FOR
THE BIG TRIP

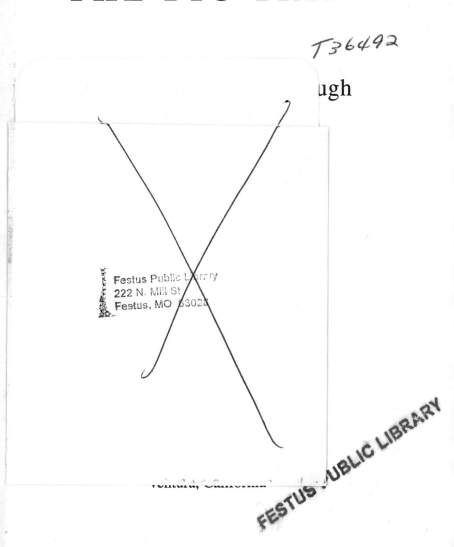

ugh

Ventura, California

PACKING FOR THE BIG TRIP

Published by:
Pathfinder Publishing of California
458 Dorothy Avenue
Ventura, CA 93003
(805) 642-9278

Library of Congress Cataloging-in-Publication Data

Walton, Charlie, 1940-
    Packing for the big trip : enhancing your life through awarness of death / by Charlie Walton.
        p. cm.
    Includes bibliographical references and index.
    ISBN 0-934793-63-8 (pbk.)
    1. Death. 2. Walton, Charlie, 1940- . 3. Conduct of life.
I. Walton, Charlie, 1940- . II. Title.
    BD444.W337 1997
    128'.5--dc21   96-45354
                                                         CIP

DEDICATION

For Jennifer

CONTENTS

1

THANK YOU, JENNIFER

About one-fifteen on a spring afternoon... things got a whole lot better for Jennifer. She finally won the war she had been fighting with her body. Cancer had been clobbering Jennifer's body with pain for over a year. It had stolen her hair... and her leg... and her mobility... and finally her breath. But it "never laid a glove on" the inner person that *was* Jennifer.

Through the years, I've been personally acquainted with a number of people who were acclaimed as spiritual thinkers and leaders. None of their eloquent talks or books inspired me as much as a few quiet conversations with Jennifer, a slight teenage girl who didn't quite make it to high school graduation... yet deserved a Ph.D. with honors in the subjects of life and death.

Jennifer would be quite embarrassed to hear me say these kinds of things about her... if... she were still listening through the ears she used to use. But I am confident that the much superior ears Jennifer now uses have placed my words in a new and more acceptable frame of reference for her.

Jennifer's new perspective on things should make it clear to her that I'm not just slinging around a bunch of sticky-sweet words for the purpose of eulogy. With her new insight, Jennifer is now able to understand that the impressions she made on me really did change my life. Changed my life for the better. Changed my life in a way that compels me to share some of those new understandings with you.

Jennifer's frank and unvarnished perception of the relationship between life and death brought into clear focus for me some concepts which have been occupying more and more space in my own brain as my years and life experiences have accumulated. Conversations with Jennifer helped to focus for me the importance of death as a topic for daily conversation. You and I *need* to be talking with each other about death... even when no one we know is sick and no one we know has recently died.

Jennifer's calm and confident approach to death can largely be explained by the fact that she had grown up in a family of faith. At home and at church, Jennifer and her sisters had heard all their lives about eternity in heaven with a loving heavenly Father. It was not just talk but sincere belief... and the depth of it was fully demonstrated in Jennifer's departure for parts unknown but optimistically anticipated.

This book, however, is not just a rah-rah piece for those who possess confident opinions about life after death. It is a book with a message about the implications that awareness of death can have on our behaviors while we live. Whether you anticipate life after death or assume that everything ends at the grave, this book proposes that leveling with yourself and your loved ones about death is one of the most productive steps toward adding peace and power to your life.

In earlier generations, death was a natural and more accepted activity of life. People weren't whisked behind hospital curtains to die. Graves weren't dug by backhoe operators. Death's omnipresent and matter-of-fact role in life made a difference in the way people thought and lived. You and I benefit greatly when we reclaim... before the fact... a natural perception of and reaction to our own deaths.

2

PACKING FOR THE TRIP

One topic... which we humans will go all the way around the conversational block to avoid... is a topic we very much need to talk about and reconcile with our personal value systems. Getting our heads straight about death is a seldom-taken... yet completely essential... first step toward mastering life. A constant awareness of and readiness for death is a doorway to completeness and contentment in life. There are life benefits in thinking about death. We can turn death into life. As a matter of fact, we can hardly approach full mastery of our lives *until* we have come to terms with the inevitability of and the actual arrangements for our own deaths.

"You would not believe," Jennifer told me one afternoon, "the things people say and do when they come to visit me. They will talk about the beautiful day outside and how it won't be long before I'll be out there enjoying it again. They know I won't. And I know I won't. But there is something that seems to stand in the way of us talking about the fact that I won't."

I told Jennifer that I enjoy talking with people who *know* they are about to die. The ironic thing is that... while we all know that we are "terminal"... only those of us for whom doctors have reluctantly set departure dates can begin to believe we are actually about to leave this life. You can talk about your big trip to Europe for years but... the day you actually pick up the tickets from your travel agent... the nature of your travel talk changes dramatically. It's suddenly time to talk *specifics*. And the same is true of people who have been told they are about to die. They are not just shooting the breeze about generic death. They are packing for the trip.

The premise of this book... to continue the travel analogy... is that there are lots of steps you and I can take right away to improve our time in this "great departure lounge." There is a wonderful feeling of freedom to be enjoyed when we have paid the bills, stopped the newspaper, and arrived at the airport ready and prepared to leave on our trip. All items are checked off our lists. We are prepared. We sit there waiting for the flight with the exhilaration of being "caught up" and "living in the present." In the same way, clearing away the long-procrastinated items of life's unfinished business, bringing all of life's relationships up to date, and clearing the decks to live life in the present can be one of life's most liberating experiences.

I think most people's assumptions about how long before they need to start packing are short-sighted. If, for example, I ask if *you* are likely to die soon, a typical reply might be, "Well, I certainly *could*... since any of us can check out at any time... but 'the good book' does talk about a full life of three-score-and-ten years and I'm sort of expecting to make it at least that far since I come from a gene pool of fairly long livers... and also... modern science keeps coming up with new things to help us all live longer and longer. In fact, I was just reading about a Japanese gentleman who lived to be 121. That would make middle age begin about 60... wouldn't it?"

Statistics can be comforting. We usually memorize the ones we like and skim over the ones we don't like. But statistics are inevitably irrelevant since *your* life is a control group of one... a control group that is highly subject to runaway buses and runaway viruses. The professional actuaries may gather around your coffin with their charts and graphs to explain why they guessed wrong about your ability to survive the freak accident that canceled your life... but your interest in their excuses will have lapsed. Mayflies almost never live longer than a day. Arctic clams live quietly underwater for 200 years or more. Yet, the length of your life has absolutely nothing to do with either of those statistics.

The bottom line is that our deaths are *imminent*. Of course, they may remain imminent for years and years. But... however long we remain busily occupied here in the waiting room... our *quality* of life is going to be tied directly to the degree to which our "philosophy of life" includes a "philosophy of death."

An honest perception of life and death has the ability to change what many consider life's ultimate catastrophe into one of life's most creative and constructive motivaters. Depending upon their perceptions of life and death... and the relationship of each to the other... some persons have been surprised to find that a physician's pronouncement of death on the horizon actually became the beginning of a period of heightened life *quality* in the face of diminishing life *quantity*.

Even though we often say that the only two certainties of life are death and taxes, we still manage to blot taxes out of our minds until April 15th looms on the horizon. Death gets equal treatment... gaining only our brief attention when a public tragedy swats us across the heart or a personal acquaintance shocks us by his or her unexpected exit. Even then, we hold the reality of our *own* deaths at arm's length and try not to let death's close calls pierce our inner armor. As one person told me, "Well, sure... I know death is out there for me. There's no denying that it's a fact of life... no pun intended. But... since there's nothing I can do about it... I figure the less I think about it, the better."

You may be thinking that person's attitude sounds perfectly reasonable. You may prefer the philosophy expressed by one person who said, "Any day I wake up on the green side of the grass, I think it's a good day." Perhaps you are even wondering, "Why would anybody intentionally write a whole book about death? Why dwell on such a *morbid* topic if you don't have to?"

The answer is... "because it's true." The death rate in your neighborhood is 100 percent. If the rate of kitchen fires in your neighborhood were 100 percent, there would be all kinds of attention given to fire prevention and, more importantly, fire readiness. Because cholesterol is true, heart patients need to know about it. Because lung cancer is true, smokers need to know about it. Because lay-offs and retirement are realities, the gainfully employed need to be alert and preparing for them. We expect local government to hire, equip, and train peace officers long before the peace is in jeopardy. We nourish our personal friendships for years before the arrival of those sudden life emergencies when we have to "be there for each other." When we save for rainy days and buy groceries before we get hungry, people chalk it up to good sense and preparedness... rather than being morbid and dwelling on negative topics.

Death awareness is a good thing. In our society... where counselors keep telling us that we need to be honest with ourselves... it's time for each of us to sit down and think carefully through the "before, during and after" of our deaths so we can begin enjoying the *life* benefits of having done so. In a society where we discuss our hemorrhoids and hangups on every daily talk show, it's time for us to declare our "death plans" as appropriate for conversation as our "vacation plans."

The surest proof of this need is that husbands and wives can talk to each other for years and then the surviving spouse is left with absolutely no idea what the dearly departed might have wanted to happen at the funeral. Families buy life insurance and faithfully make payments on it for years... but try to locate the life insurance papers or the insurance agent's phone number after the family record-keeper dies.

Death awareness doesn't mean we drape the house in black and sit in darkened rooms waiting for the end. Quite the contrary, it may mean that we drape the house in bright colors and throw the big party that we've been putting off for so long. Thinking seriously about death can result in all sorts of wonderful new priorities for life. Death awareness is about living.

3

THE DEATH RATE IS 100 PERCENT

Years ago, I heard about the tombstone of a teenager in a New England cemetery. The inscription on it was reputed to be: "This is exactly what I expected... but not this soon."

That's the way it is with death. We know it's coming, but its arrival is always a shock. No matter how sick somebody is... no matter how dangerously they may be living... we are always shocked when we hear that they have died. Are we more surrounded by death and destruction than ever before? It certainly seems that way if you go to the movies or watch the news. A voice from the radio told me recently that this year more Americans will die of cancer than in all the wars we've fought in our nation's history. And... while that's a pretty shocking statistic... death is *not* really more prevalent than it used to be. It just gets a lot more *coverage* than before. Death has been equally prevalent in every century... since it is impossible to exceed 100 percent.

There is an old Buddhist parable about the prevalence of death. The story describes a woman who could not accept the death of her young son. She went about crying out for someone to bring the boy back to life. She begged Buddha to perform a miracle. He agreed to heal the boy if the woman would bring him a handful of mustard seeds collected door-to-door. Buddha's stipulation, however, was that the woman could only collect mustard seeds from families that had not been touched by death. Her door-to-door efforts yielded not one mustard seed. The woman soon realized the universality of death and was able to give up her false hopes and proceed with her own natural work of grief.

When we consider the intricacies of our bodies, we ought to be more surprised that we keep living. All those millions of heartbeats and breaths. All those chemicals that have to arrive at just the right glands at just the right times. If we considered the odds, it should shock us to wake up *alive* every morning. But most of us have been doing it for so long that we take it for granted. On the other hand, if you hang around long enough, somebody you know is going to die. And... the more people you know... the more encounters you are likely to have with death.

Somebody has to become your first occasion to hear about death. Aunt Maggie was the first person I knew who died. Of course, there were pets that died and Roy Rogers and Gene Autry killed off a respectable number of bad guys at the movie matinee every Saturday... but Aunt Maggie was the first person I remember being personally acquainted with before she changed from alive to dead.

Aunt Maggie wasn't really my Aunt. She was my Dad's aunt but everybody in the family called her Aunt Maggie. I have no way of guessing how old that lady was. She had gray hair all the time I knew her so that put her in the automatic category of "old" for me. For a kid my age, there were only two age groups. There were kids... and there were people who were old.

Though Aunt Maggie was old, she had a redeeming characteristic. She liked kids. So, she not only remembered my name from one family reunion to the next... she also expressed sincere interest in whatever I was interested in at the time. It was enough to make me consider adding a third age category called "old people who seem to be interested in kids."

Sometime before she died, Aunt Maggie had surgery for varicose veins. After her recovery... I was the lucky kid who received all her unused elastic bandages. Since elastic bandages are a most wonderful gift for a kid with an active imagination, I thought about Aunt Maggie even more often than I saw her... which was normally at Thanksgiving dinner, Christmas dinner, and the annual summer picnic.

I don't know how old Aunt Maggie was when she died. I don't know what killed her. Cancer's probably a safe guess. It was long enough ago that people didn't talk about causes of death. Grown-ups whispered about it. Little kids like me just found out that the nice lady who gave them the elastic bandages had died.

My parents and I went to the funeral home. I saw Aunt Maggie in her casket... looking all powdered up and sleeping on a satin pillow. We went to the cemetery and I was fascinated by the tent canopy and the deep hole and the way the pall bearers let the casket slowly down into the ground. They filled the hole with dirt and we all went home. It was a lot like church: you dress up... you sit quietly while the grown-ups use a lot of big words and long sentences... and then you go home and play with your elastic bandages.

Aunt Maggie's *death* and my *life* seemed to be topics with absolutely no connection. One was an activity that goes with being old. The other was a matter of running and playing and going to the movies on Saturday. That was probably the way my parents hoped it would go for me: a natural, arms-length encounter with one of life's important formalities... but without undue emphasis on the morbid to create even the slightest emotional ripple for an impressionable youngster.

The trouble with death is... it has a way of popping up in your life and happening to people who aren't on schedule for dying as Aunt Maggie seemed to be. When I was in the fourth grade, there was a cute little girl that I was desperately in "like" with. One day, the teacher announced that the little girl's father had been killed by lightning on the golf course. I had met her father. He didn't seem old. He could actually talk to a fourth grader. How could he be dead?

Death got even closer a few years later. One of my buddies all through elementary school and into high school never came back from summer vacation. He and a friend were shooting tin cans off a fence post with a .22 rifle. He reached back for the rifle to take his turn. It went off. The bullet pierced his heart. He died in the car on the way to the hospital. His parents donated a big clock for the front of the school building... and while it ticked... life went on for the rest of us.

That same year, there was a handsome young football hero in our high school who died of a brain hemorrhage when he came back to play too soon after a concussion. His doctor had said everything would be okay as long as he wore the specially padded helmet. He wore the helmet but everything wasn't okay. They rushed him to the hospital in the middle of the second half. He lingered long enough for all of us to be tearful and prayerful. Then he died. His football jersey and his photograph were placed in the trophy case. The rest of us passed by that trophy case every day on the way to class as life went on.

After that, our student body made it a couple of years with no sudden deaths. Then, Odell was killed on his motorcycle. In his black leather jacket and motorcycle boots, Odell was everyone's favorite bad boy around the school. With a ready smile and a twinkle in his eye, Odell seemed to be able to get away with cutting more classes than he attended. More than anything else, Odell loved riding that motorcycle... the one he wrapped around a tree after midnight one weekend. We were all shocked. We were all sorry. We were all being reminded again that *death can happen to people who are not old.*

Frank was a kid I had known since elementary school. His real name was Francis but we called him Frank. After elementary school, Frank went off to a private high school. I didn't see him again until we turned up at the same college. Though Frank was an intelligent person and a talented artist, he was one who seemed to have a need to be different from whatever group was around him.

Frank earned a reputation for nonconformity and wore it with pride. Then... not long before he would have graduated... Frank learned that he had terminal cancer. He took it in stride... even shocked a lot of us by how matter-of-factly he talked about the progressions of the disease that was taking his life.

The stories of his pranks in the hospital filtered back to us at school. Everybody's favorite story was about the time Frank got a new roommate in the middle of the night. A man who had gone through emergency surgery was wheeled into Frank's room to recover. In the dim light of the hospital room, the poor guy came out of his anesthesia to find Frank standing over him wearing a white gown and folding his hands in prayer. "Greetings, my son," said Frank in his most angelic voice. "You came to us here during the night."

Frank eventually died. They put a special page for him in the year book. We were sorry that Frank was not graduating with us. But we didn't think about him very long. We had jobs to find... marriages to make... families to begin.

In my early thirties, I shared an office for a few weeks with a guy named Larry. He had completed his college and Army years with an impressive resume and the organization I worked for was excited to have him come on board. Larry was a real catch and everyone expected great things from him. But it didn't take long in a shared office for me to see that Larry had a pretty twisted view of life. He began to tell me about voices that informed him of secret government conspiracies. Within a few weeks, Larry had flown into a rage, had violently attacked another staff member whom he suspected of being a Communist spy, and had run screaming from the building. The next we heard, Larry had run afoul of the police, been placed in the psychiatric ward of the hospital, been released on his own recognizance, and shot himself to death on the fourth of July. Larry came and went and none of us even knew when or where his funeral took place.

When I was in my mid-thirties, there was another wake-up call from death. George and I went way back. We had known each other through college, then graduate school, and eventually had become good friends all over again ten years later in another city. George decided to have some elective surgery for an old knee injury that had bothered him for years. The surgery went fine but... while he was recovering at home... a blood clot broke loose and ended George's life within a matter of seconds. When we heard the news, my middle son said what all of us were feeling. "But how can *he* be dead?" Tim marveled. "He wasn't *old*!"

Those were painfully prophetic words to come out of Tim's mouth. A week after his own twenty-second birthday, Tim and his younger brother, Don, and Don's best friend, Bryan, would all three be dead... victims of carbon monoxide poisoning from sitting in a car with a bad muffler on a cold December night. After a lifetime of paying close attention to the deaths of acquaintances, I was finally face-to-face with the death of someone who was an integral part of my life.

I didn't write this chapter just to tell you that I've known a lot of people who died. This chapter is here because... more than likely... there was an Aunt Maggie in your young life.

And a schoolmate's parent who died. And it is a rare graduating class that hasn't lost its own Odell to a grinding road crash... or its own Frank to cancer.

The more years you live... and the more friends you have... the more certain it is that you are going to face the shocking death of a friend or acquaintance. When your wake-up calls occur, you can either take them to heart... or... change the subject. All of us who are living are being exposed to a daily gold mine of life's educational experiences. Unfortunately, not all of us are paying attention.

Getting the message from deaths that occur around you is something you have to *decide* to do. All the encouragement we get from our society is in the opposite direction... away from thoughtfulness. "Why think about death... it's way out in the future." "Change the subject... nobody wants to hear that unhappy stuff." "Get on with your life... fill up on trivia and forget the meaningful." "Accentuate the positive... eliminate the negative." We live in a death-denying society.

Death is not a four-letter word. There is tremendous life value to be gained by dealing head-on with the *certainty* of your own death... the *inevitability* of your own death... the potential *immediacy* of your own death... even the *positive potential* of your own death. Considering these things and taking care in advance of the adjustments they dictate can make you a happier, more mature person. But... to gain all the positive life benefits of death awareness... you will have to make yourself one of earth's minority... one of those few who are determined enough to swim upstream in order to make the most of their lives... and their deaths.

4

THE ELEPHANT IN
THE LIVING ROOM

Most of the twelve-step addiction programs like to tell the story of the elephant in the living room. It is a wonderful analogy... one that families of addicts seem to identify with immediately. Its concept is that living with the secret of a family member's addiction is like living in a house where nobody mentions the fact that there is an elephant in the living room.

It is tragically hilarious to picture family members climbing over and around a giant pachyderm... reaching under its great belly to serve coffee to visitors... pushing the huge trunk out of the way as they watch television... all the while pretending that everything is normal. If you were to ask them about the elephant in the living room, they would look at you quizzically and ask, "What elephant?"

Death has become an elephant in the living room of our society. Each of us is hopelessly addicted to death and yet we persist in pretending that it does not exist. Entire cultures teach succeeding generations to "keep a stiff upper lip," "look on the sunny side," "hope for the best," and "never say die" when facing the impending death of a loved one. Soldiers go off to war whistling and making jovial small talk to avoid discussing the obvious fact that war is quite simply the business of hastening the unavoidable.

If you happen to make your living writing advertising copy or television commercials, you are told early in your career that... while getting attention and motivating people are your missions... the ultimate attention-getter and the most powerful motivator are off limits for you. Death is on the taboo list. It is not to be mentioned in anything you write.

Perhaps our taboo about "death in advertising"... (sounds strangely like "truth in advertising" doesn't it?)... results from the fact that generating a desire for the shiny items that advertisers are trying to sell requires an assumption of uninterrupted life and permanence. Even life insurance commercials emphasize the stability of their companies and the happiness of their beneficiaries while carefully tip-toeing around the simple fact that their products are matters of death.

The last thing most advertisers want to do in their ads is remind potential consumers of their temporary natures or of the ultimately inconsequential nature of the products they are pushing. For years, automobile advertisers avoided talking about car safety features. They were afraid that the mention of seat belts and air bags might remind buyers of their mortality and convince them to make the old car last a little longer. Once government regulations required seat belts and air bags, automobile advertising started to mention them as features.

If you are thinking as you read this that you have recently begun to see ads that *do* talk about death, you are right. Unprecedented advertising challenges like the mushrooming statistics of drunk driving, the insidious sale of deadly drugs, and the steadily rising death toll of AIDS have caused the ad makers to lift the age-old taboo. When the only influence you have with your target audience is the fear of dying, that is the theme you must use. The unfortunate thing is that we have waited until fear of dying is the last resort. There are many messages that might be enhanced by honest... not ominous... mention of the inevitability of death.

One of the most persuasive pieces of advertising copy I ever wrote was for a client who wanted to get people to sign up for a Bible correspondence course. On one side of a simple postage-paid reply card we printed the following words:

The hand with which you hold this card, and the eye with which you see it, will die someday. But the spirit by which you evaluate these words will never die.

In view of the brevity of life and the length of eternity, the wise person makes preparations. In eternal matters, only the word of God is conclusive. You owe it to yourself to know the Bible.

As a study aid, a free Bible course is available to you by correspondence. Even the postage is paid for you. This undenominational course teaches no man-made creed... just the Bible.

It was stark copy, pulled no punches, and was quite successful in the number of responses it generated. It seemed to me to be the kind of approach required to grab readers' attention and focus it on their mortal and immortal natures.

In a follow-up project, my client decided to use the same approach in a series of newspaper ads. The ad agency they approached to develop the theme was aghast at the wording and eventually talked the client into *softening* the approach because, as they put it, "the first rule of advertising is to avoid unpleasant subjects like death."

But it is not just in our commercial communications that we refuse to say what we really mean. In private and intimate conversations between spouses, lovers, and life-long friends, we still find ways to say it without saying it. We would rather wax poetic and say that someone has "gone to sleep" than to admit that they have died. We speak of them "passing away," or "passing over," or simply "passing" rather than using the word that is so hard to form with our mouths. Funeral homes now have "slumber parlors" and "reposing rooms" where we go to view bodies and "coaches" instead of hearses for funeral processions to follow.

If you have lived through the painful grief process that follows the death of a loved one, you probably recall the first time you tried to actually *say* that they had died. More than likely, you had been dealing with the fact of it for a while. You may even have made it through the funeral and related activities but... not until that moment... had you actually come face to face with the "D-word." Perhaps you were talking with a new acquaintance. And, as you explained what had happened, you began to realize that the D-word was looming up at the end of your sentence. Your mind kept telling you that there was no reason that you should not be able to say that word. But... when the moment arrived... your voice simply disappeared and your composure broke. The words "died" and "dead" refused to be uttered... even though they were absolute, undeniable truth. You almost felt that your loved one would not be fully dead until the moment you heard the word coming from your own mouth.

One very realistic Christian widow remarked to me that it always struck her as curious when people said that she had "lost" her husband. She had not lost the man, she explained. She knew exactly where he was. "His shell was in a box underground at the cemetery and his soul had moved into another dimension to be with God." Her choice of words may make us flinch initially but her grasp of the situation and her policy of "truth in description" certainly leaves less room for denial and self-deception.

Equally beneficial honesty could be expressed by a spouse who had no belief in life after death. "We had wonderful years together but... now that death has intervened... I will treasure the memories and proceed with life as this one who was part of me would have wished me to."

One of my favorite acquaintances spent many years of his life as a medical missionary in Nigeria. Not only was his dedication inspiring, but he also had a habit of straight talk that could be provocative and sometimes humorous. I heard him tell once about the private conference he routinely conducted with patients on the night before their surgeries. He would go to the bedside of a patient and confide, "You know... all my patients die." Just as the shocked patient was ready to call off the surgery and go running out of the hospital, the doctor would add with a smile, "Of course, most of them live for years after I operate on them... but eventually... they *all* die."

From that beginning, the good doctor would proceed with a heart-to-heart talk about their fears, their confidences, and their religious faith or lack of it. He led many people to faith during his years in Africa and, no doubt, changed the short- and long-term futures of many. Any of his patients who did happen to die in surgery were certainly not taken by surprise as they entered the next stage of their lives. And those who came through the surgery and lived for years afterward had received a valuable reality check compliments of this physician who laid it on the line.

Most modern doctors, however, seem to be taught to use any words except the obvious ones. "It's only a matter of time now" is a humorous euphemism of modern medicine that leaves us wondering what it was "a matter of" before. "The patient has expired" makes us anticipate some elaboration on the metaphor like "and is no longer under warranty." "The patient is on his last leg" creates a mental picture that is far more humorous than it is helpful.

Perhaps one of our most tragic ways of looking at death is epitomized in the statement that "the patient appears to be losing the battle." This, no doubt, arises from the medical world's total emphasis on sustaining physical life at all costs. But "*losing* the battle" places an inaccurate and disappointing value on the realities of the end of life. The real truth is quite the opposite of "losing the battle." Patients who have endured tremendous pain and suffering in the final stages of their hospitalizations could more appropriately be said to have "*won* the battle" when they are finally able to take leave of their tortured bodies. Whether they proceed into life after death or into the final release of oblivion, they have won the battle.

If we are determined to find other words, let us do our searching on the *positive* side of the language. Jennifer's father opened the memorial service for his courageous daughter by saying, "Her faith has prevailed." Albert Schweitzer once spoke of one of his friends who had died while he was away in Africa. Schweitzer's very positive euphemism was: "And, when I returned home, she had gone over to the majority." There is nothing wrong with euphemisms. In fact, they are especially effective at revealing our fears or our confidences. Some euphemisms reveal the conviction that death is the end of everything but memories. Other sets of words demonstrate confidence and conviction that death is the beginning of better things to follow.

People of the Christian faith traditionally use a number of positive ways to say "death" without using the word. They often speak of believers who have "crossed the river" or been "called home" or "gone to live with Jesus." These can be poetic and supportive elaborations on the simple fact that the person has died. But they have their dangers. There is always a chance that speakers and listeners are not dealing with exactly the same images and will end up communicating unintended messages. When we are using euphemisms, we need to make sure that they are for the purpose of elaboration and elucidation... and not just to keep from admitting that death has taken place.

Especially when children are among the listeners is there a danger that some of our flowery explanations might be taken literally and prove confusing or even threatening. In an era when enlightened parents would not think of telling a child that the stork delivers babies, there remain parents who will go to great lengths to shield a child from the language of *natural* death. And this... in a time when the media make the most of every aspect of *unnatural* death. Television news has been accused of selecting stories by the rule: "If it bleeds, it leads." I heard about one little girl who was such a product of the television age that... when her mother told her that the nice old lady across the street had died... the little girl's first question was, "Who killed her?"

Our children have to learn somewhere that death is a normal, natural part of our life together. Life creates frequent opportunities for natural teaching on the subject. Who better to grasp those opportunities for matter-of-fact explanation than honest, loving parents? I have met people who were never allowed to attend a funeral until they were adults. Their parents may have thought they were protecting them... but they were really storing up emotional trauma that would eventually have to be confronted. In retrospect, I am appreciative for all the times that my parents took me along to visit a funeral home, sign the visitors' register, view a corpse, say a word of condolence to the family members, and talk quietly with friends and neighbors before leaving.

I have not yet had the chance to attend an Irish wake or a New Orleans funeral parade led by a jazz band but they sound like wonderful approaches to a fact of life. They are hold-overs from a less sophisticated and more honest time when people *celebrated* death. Earlier cultures were far ahead

of us in their healthy ways of treating death. They li
daily touch with nature and therefore knew that nothir
more natural than death. They were no doubt saddened as
they contemplated the absence of a loved one who had previ-
ously been present, but they quite naturally arrived at the assumption that the person's journey was continuing... only in
some different realm. When archaeologists open ancient
graves, they usually find skeletons surrounded by gifts and
supplies for continued existence. It is clear that those who
conducted the final rites had an idea that these rites weren't
final. And... judging by the gifts they gave... they obviously
considered "whatever came next" to be better than "whatever
came before."

Our predecessors demonstrated their clear assumption
that death was a progression to some subsequent form of life.
In my opinion, our society's loss of that assumption has made
us poorer, not richer. Our move from natural rural rituals of
death and dying... to sophisticated urban devices for glossing
over death... have left us with less ability to accept, to cope,
and to go on with life. Our modern denial of death leaves us
shocked when it occurs and quick to visit professional grief
counselors to lament that the departed "did not deserve" to
die. Perhaps the best answer I have ever heard to the com-
plaint that we do not deserve to die is a quote attributed to
Jack Benny as he accepted a prestigious award. "I don't deserve this," said Benny, "but then, I have arthritis and I don't
deserve that either."

Even into the early years of the twentieth century, people
were most likely to die at home. And, when they died, it was
a tradition for someone to walk around the house and stop the
pendulums on all the clocks... to record the time of death for
the authorities and perhaps also to indicate that the person
had moved out of a realm of time and into a realm of time-
lessness.

Today, you rarely get the chance to die at home... whispering final words to your gathered loved ones. The modern style of death calls for your last visual image to be... not the faces of loved ones... but the acoustical tile ceiling of a hospital room or a medical emergency suite... where you are surrounded by grim-faced strangers sticking needles into your body and pounding on your chest for dear life. It is an unfortunate and unnecessary vision of desperation and failure. How much better if it were a vision communicating the successful completion of one phase of existence and the loving departure for the next phase. No wonder so many people returning from "near-death experiences" describe hovering above the emergency room mob scene and wondering why those people down there kept pounding on that poor person on the table.

One reason that so many of us doubt that death will ever happen to us personally is that it never has. We've heard about it. We know it has happened to others but we all assume that death... like an accident... always happens to somebody else. We expect to be the ones who find out about other people's deaths but never to be the star in the final act of our own run just before we take our show on the road.

Only *intellectually* do you and I know we are going to die. We would answer "yes" on the test question that asks whether we believe we are going to die. But we would probably not do so well on an essay question that required us to "Describe your plans, your feelings, and your expectations of your own death." Many of us would have to just fill in "N/A" for "Not Anticipating."

5

ALL DRESSED UP AND NO PLACE TO GO?

It has only been in the last hundred years that we have lost touch with the naturalness of death as a part of life. When we built skyscrapers and interstates where the villages and farms used to be, we removed people from their connection to the land, the animals, and the natural role of death in life. Today, the closest most of us get to regaining that natural perspective of life cycles is the moment when PBS gives us an up-close-and-personal view of a hunting party of African hyenas isolating and killing a zebra colt. Momentarily, we get the idea... but soon... the staff of the PBS station returns to the screen with a fund-raising appeal and hustles us back to the assumption that human life (and pledge drives) go on forever.

In earlier centuries, poets and writers created literary classics because they not only mentioned, but dwelt upon, the certainty of death and its implications for life. Thomas

Gray called his society's attention to the inevitability of death with his "Elegy Written in a Country Churchyard." John Donne tasted deeply of the pleasures the world had to offer and then turned in bitter disillusionment against them to write classics like his "Death, Be Not Proud." Robert Herrick encouraged his readers to gather rosebuds while they had the chance since "the same flower that smiles today, tomorrow will be dying." And the common people always rushed to attend Shakespeare's plays, knowing they could count on plenty of dying at the end and a clear good-guy-bad-guy reason for each and every death.

Literary giants and preachers in high, starched collars pounded home the theme of death as the great equalizer. The rich, the poor, the famous, and the anonymous all become equal at death. As to how equal things are after death, there are wide differences of opinion.

Atheists believe that the equality all creatures share at death is *oblivion*. This belief makes for a convenient, low-maintenance philosophy of life... but one that often wears thin as death approaches. As the man said: "There are no atheists in foxholes." Toward the end of life, it becomes harder and harder to maintain that the consciousness which has "been us" all through a lifetime of experience and achievement has actually been only the result of random collisions of brain chemicals. People who are not atheists are sometimes guilty of jumping to the erroneous conclusion that... because atheists anticipate nothing beyond the grave... they automatically become money-grubbing, pleasure-seeking hedonists who live by the ancient motto of "Eat and drink for tomorrow we die" or by the more modern bumper sticker claim that "He who dies with the most toys wins." No fair. Many of our world's great humanitarians have little confidence in any existence after death. Even so, they are wise enough to realize that... regardless of what happens after death... they can find greater satisfaction this side of death by serving instead of being served.

The Hindu believes that the soul or spirit (*atman*) within him or her is part of the great world spirit (*brahman*) that exists eternally in all things. By a law (*karma*) of good or bad deeds, each soul is reborn many times on earth... receiving at each birth the animal or human body it earned in the previous life. Once a person comes to understand fully the eternal and unchangeable soul, he or she is ready to break out of the relentless cycle of birth, death, and rebirth. Release (*moksha*) from the reincarnation cycle occurs when a soul finally grasps eternal truth, understanding, and bliss sufficiently to no longer need to be born again. A person reaches this breakout point by dedication to yoga and meditation, by learning to love with the whole heart, or by working selflessly for the good of others.

The followers of Gautama Buddha believe that... instead of an eternal soul (*atman*)... each person has a "not-self" or "non-soul" (*anatman*). Gautama did not believe that any part of us would survive death, change, and decay. He compared the "I" to the *sound* of a lute... meaning that the sound is not the strings, not the wood, not any part of the lute... but the *audible* result of all the lute's parts working together. By analogy, "we" are the results of our bodily components working together so... when our components are gone... so are we. Since Buddha saw no eternal essence in humans, he taught his followers to meditate their way toward *nirvana*, a state of absolute peace right here in the midst of our chaotic world. If a Buddhist keeps meditating until he or she finally sees things as they truly are, he or she is ready to leave behind the normal concerns and graspings of human life... become completely selfless... and move into a sort of immune-to-the-pain-of-death realm right in the middle of life. The first *nirvana* is death to selfishness. The next stage, the *parinirvana,* includes the death of the body as well.

Jewish doctrine rarely mentions the afterlife but places emphasis on living *this* life fully and well. While almost all Jews speak of continuing after death in the memories of their friends and loved ones, Jewish anticipations about the afterlife range from reincarnation... to resurrection... to oblivion. A ceremonial prayer called the *kaddish* is repeated by the Jewish family throughout the first year after a loved one's death. Then, after the first year, the *kaddish* is repeated once a year on the anniversary of the death. While the *kaddish* praises God and requests "peace from heaven" and the "gift of life," Jews usually have very little to say publicly about life beyond the grave.

Muslims believe strongly in a cataclysmic end of this world, followed by a day of judgment which will begin an afterlife of either paradise or punishment. Those who have lead lives of obedience and have represented *Allah* well on earth will be rewarded eternally. For those who have lived selfishly and refused to honor *Allah* with their lives, punishment will be swift, sure, but not necessarily eternal. Between death and the Muslim judgment, there is a time of waiting which will be harder for some than for others. Only those who have been martyred for their faith or have died in a holy war (*jihad*) get to skip the time of waiting and go directly into paradise. Muslim descriptions of the final judgment place the emphasis on the simple weighing of a life's good versus its evil... with no anticipation of mercy.

Christians hold that, when they die, they move into a realm where the things of earth no longer matter. Much of Christian teaching, in fact, encourages believers to get a head start by living according to "after-death values" even while they are still occupying space here on earth. Among Christians, there are differing degrees of faith in eternal life. Some believe strongly. Others assume that, if the church believes it, they eventually will. But central to Christian faith is the idea that God became a human and lived on the earth as Jesus

Christ. Christians take courage from their belief that... before Jesus left the earth to return to God... he destroyed the power of death by his resurrection from the grave. Most Christians believe that Jesus' words were as much for them as for his Galilean listeners when he promised, "Because I live, you also will live." Christians believe that Jesus' resurrection changed death from a *wall*... into a *door*... and that Jesus' intercessions at the judgment will allow the faithful to be saved in spite of their failures and imperfections.

The preceding summaries of religious beliefs are all obvious oversimplifications. It is almost a certainty that one branch or another of each religious group will take issue with the beliefs attributed to it. For the purposes of this chapter, it is adequate to say in summary that... as we progress through our lives... we all go through philosophical changes and opinions about what is going to happen after we die. If religious doctrines and affiliations don't change our minds, the simple process of getting older (i.e. closer to death itself) certainly does.

The longer you live, the more opportunities death has to brush against your life. The closer it strikes to you and the more times you see it take people who can only be described as "innocent bystanders," the more lasting impression it should make on you. Perhaps you remember the story of the overprotective parent who sent a note to her first-grader's teacher on the first day of school... a note saying, "Robbie is such a sensitive child that... if he should do anything wrong... please slap the child next to him... and Robbie will get the message."

Many of us live very self-centered and self-protective lives. Time after time, death slaps the person or the family next to us but we fail to transfer the message to ourselves. We remain convinced that death is something that happens to other people and that their trials exist primarily as backdrops and supporting plots to our own lives which are, we assume, at center stage of the world's interest.

Our assumption pendulum, however, swings to the opposite extreme when someone very close to us dies. Then... instead of the common assumption that accidents and illnesses happen only in other people's families... we begin to obsessively *expect* tragedies to strike us at any moment. In the months after our two sons died, I shuddered every time my remaining son or my wife went out of my sight. Intellectually, I knew that the odds of an accident happening to them were no greater than they had ever been. But emotionally, I was certain that they would never make it back home alive.

The first time that Kay was nearly an hour late getting home from a meeting, I sat at my desk, staring into space, and waiting for the policeman to pull into the drive and tell me that she had died in an accident. She finally arrived home and could not understand why I was so over-wrought. She had intended to call and say she would be late but became preoccupied about something and it slipped her mind. The time passed before she knew it. The time didn't pass before I knew it! In my imagination I was already living the first days of my life without her.

The news media remind us in daily and graphic detail that there are lots of new ways to die... ways that have not been a part of our world since the lawless era of Dodge City and Boot Hill. You don't have to know the victims personally. You simply relate to the fact that they were killed even while taking every measure they knew to stay out of harm's way. On a busy street. In broad daylight. Unprovoked incidents. They gave the assailant everything demanded and still lost their lives.

A friend told me of a business assignment that required him to visit several inner city schools. In nearly every building, he saw memorials in the halls... memorials to students who had been killed in drive by shootings. Some had wandered innocently into the crossfire of automatic weapons as drug dealers negotiated turf ownership.

One day as I toured an electric power plant on a writing assignment, the man assigned to escort me said casually, "Yep... there's a hundred ways to get killed in a power plant." He proceeded to describe a number of accidental deaths from the plant's past... like the employee who was killed instantly when he walked unsuspectingly into an invisible stream of superheated steam. My escort's *intent* was to impress me with the safety consciousness required of people who work in power plants. His *result* was that I have often recalled his statement in many other times and places. And it's true: there *are* a hundred ways to get killed in almost any arena of modern life.

It is curious how some deaths grab our attention and others miss us completely. The news reports a housefire far from where you live and it's just another item of news. But let a housefire of the same scope occur one street over from yours and you are among the mourners at the funeral and the willing organizers of the relief effort. Five hundred North Americans a day die of lung cancer and it never makes the news. But... if 200 people perish in an airplane crash... it stops us in our tracks.

Our sympathy, our attention, and our aid are not determined by the numbers involved in a tragedy, the types of death described, or even our ability to help. We live daily with the news of death. Some accounts grab us by the heart. Others never phase us. What is the difference? What is it that causes one family's suffering to become your suffering while many others leave you unaffected?

Perhaps the most common factor of human empathy is familiarity with the experience that the sufferers are going through. If it is "someone like you," there is immediate and sincere interest and concern. If it is someone in your occupation or your building, there is more than passive attention to the details of the unfortunate incident.

All my life I had flipped past newspaper accounts of automobile accidents that had taken the lives of teenagers. But... when my own boys died in an automobile... I was destined never to skip lightly over those stories again. Now... when I see such an story... I already know the look of the cluttered room left by the young one who died... and in my mind I can clearly hear the anguished sobs that fill the house.

The primary message of this book is that... regardless of what you think is going to happen *after* you die... paying more attention to the certainty of and potential immediacy of your death can improve what happens to you *before* you die. Experience has taught me that a heightened awareness of death is a major key to the enhancement of life.

6

A BETTER PLACE TO BE?

In every age there seems to be a natural and continuing interest in what happens after death. Part of our makeup as human beings is that we don't like puzzles without solutions. We want the answers in the back of the book. We want mystery writers to solve everything and wrap it all up with a neat twist before the end of the story. We may be willing to struggle for a while assembling the pieces of a coffee table puzzle... but before long... we're ready for our host or hostess to tell us how it's done... show us how it works... give us the solution so we can put it behind us.

The frustrating thing about death is that none of the real experts on the topic have come back to tell us how it ends. Even those few who write accounts of their near-death experiences have to admit that they were only *near* death... they didn't follow through to the end of the process. It reminds me of a person I met in New Zealand who told me immediately that he did not like the United States. "Have you been to the United States?" I naturally asked. "Yes," he replied, "When I was on the ship from England to New Zealand, we stopped over for a day in Miami and I found that I did not like your country!"

We are being equally ridiculous if we base all our expectations about the afterlife on the testimonies of those who have had near-death experiences. We would not consider a person to be a Disney World expert who had only set one foot inside the front gate of the Magic Kingdom... but we do seem willing to latch onto confident near-death descriptions as complete answers to the puzzle of what happens after we die. I think we have to be wiser than to accept the classic "long tunnel, bright light, and white-suited figures" as anything approaching a complete description.

Our relationship to the life to come can be fittingly compared to the relationship that a human fetus has to its birth. Picture yourself having a conversation with a fetus who is lounging comfortably in the mother's womb. You are trying to describe the beautiful and exciting experiences waiting just at the other end of the birth canal. You say to the fetus, "I'm telling you... you cannot imagine all the wonderful things waiting for you as soon as you are born. Just wait until you taste some chocolate... or feel the warmth of sunshine... or experience the joy of human love. Life after birth can be absolutely wonderful!"

The fetus leans back in the comfort of the womb and responds, "Maybe you are right and maybe you are not. How am I to know that there's anything at all out there? I can't see it from here. And... even if there *is* life after birth... I can hardly believe that it could be any better than what I've got here. I am warm and cozy. I have all the oxygen and nourishment I need. What could be better than just dozing and growing and floating here in the comforts of my womb? And besides... between me and that wonderful life you keep talking about is a step that scares me a lot. I can tell from here that the birth process is no picnic... considering that tiny opening I'm expected to squeeze through. All the blood and pain and... I don't know... birth may be too big a price to pay for the life you are describing. Why would I want to leave here for an unknown realm?"

Some births are easier than others and some ways of dying are easier than others. Transitions from womb-to-nursery and from life-to-afterlife occur with relative ease for some and with great pain and difficulty for others. But... even as the pain of a difficult delivery is soon forgotten amid the rejoicing that a new life has entered the world... so the agony of the most painful death will fade amid the wonders of the next life... a realm in which things are better than anything we've ever known before. We struggle through birth. We struggle through death. Only afterward can we understand why it was worth the struggle.

At this point, any reader who is uncomfortable with the preceding talk about "wonders of the next life" may be thinking, "That's fine for people who believe in it... but what about those of us who can't honestly see how there can be anything after this body dies?"

One certainty is that none of us possesses certainty about what happens after death. One person's guess is as valid as another's. Some groups like to refer to their guesses by the dignified name of "faith"... but until that faith becomes sight... until they see it happen... they must admit that they are in fact only guessing. It is so unfortunate when we fall into the trap of equating our "faith" with "fact." Faith may be strongly believed and confidently held but it is by definition still faith... still an opinion... still a guess.

My guess... is that the *continuation* of life is rather more natural and likely than the *cessation* of it. To me, the most positive evidence in this *world-we-know* of a *world-to-come* is the relationship that each of us maintains with his or her own spirit. Think of the spirit that has been "you" since your first memories... has changed and grown through all your life experiences... and remains "you" even as you read these words. It becomes harder and harder as you grow older to believe that the "spirit that is you" and all the relationships that are interwoven with that spirit are simply the result of random collisions of chemicals in your brain... collisions that will cease when your brain dies. We are quite aware of and frequently communicate about our spirits that won't go away. Even while we live, our spirits are able to take flight via music, literature, or conversation and exist in far flung realms beyond our own physical limits. Why should it trouble us to think that our spirits might go rambling even farther afield once they are released from these bodies that cannot fly?

So... it is my present opinion that life is forever and that much of our confusion about the subject occurs when we assume that life has *ended* simply because it suddenly *changes* into a form that we can no longer see with human eyes. Our society constantly confuses bodies with identities. Thinking that people *are* what they look like, we paint and pamper our shells trying to spruce up the person inside. Eventually, we realize that the only way to make the body look its very best is to renovate the spirit within that body. Make the person happy and that person's mobile container will take on a much more pleasing appearance... a radiance that can never be achieved through make-up.

Even after death, the morticians bring in hairdressers and make-up artists to try and give the look of life to our empty containers. It's not an easy job. As soon as the heart stops beating, the skin automatically takes on a pallor that characterizes a body minus its living person. Muscles have no tone. Lungs have no air. There is no longer the vibrant fullness of a life within. The body literally shrinks and becomes measurably smaller than it was when it had a living person inside.

In the midst of all the sorrow and grief of the funeral home, a very important transition is taking place in the minds of those who stand next to the coffin... gazing at the lifeless expression... and touching the cold, unresponsive hands. Those mourners are coming to the essential understanding that the person they knew so well is *no longer in that body*. The cosmetologists may have done wonderful work but that face will never again be the face they knew because it no longer has that one-of-a-kind person inside... altering its moods and expressions and giving life to those now flat features.

But... if we are going to a better place... what is that place like? Our human desire to eliminate unsolved problems and unanswered questions keeps demanding a full explanation. To simply say that it will be *better* fails to satisfy. But... if we recall the analogy of explaining life to the unborn fetus... we begin to see that we are constitutionally unable to comprehend any accurate description that might be given us since we exist in one world and the life-to-come exists in another.

To me, a most basic principle of communication is that no person can comprehend a thing that he or she has not experienced. Even familiarity with a few aspects of a thing can help us begin to grasp it. For example, if you are describing for me a "red and green rock eater" I can put together a relatively close mental picture even though I've never seen one. I can imagine it since I have experienced (1) red, (2) green, (3) rocks, and (4) the eating process. But... if you are describing for me a "robanlish crantofler"... I am at a complete loss to visualize it. I have never seen a crantofler... and if I had... I still would have no idea how a robanlish crantofler might differ from any other crantofler. We earth-bound folk are no more able to understand and value the heavenly concepts of perpetual light, absolute contentment, and eternal worship than the fetus in the womb is able to understand ice hockey.

Much as we may wish to understand everything in advance, some understandings are impossible for us. All concepts of the future are grasped and held by faith. For Christians, the Bible promises in First Corinthians that "... no eye has seen, no ear has heard, no mind has conceived what God has prepared for those who love him." Add to that some of the final words of Jesus to his disciples when he said in John, chapter fourteen, "I go to prepare a place for you... and if I go... I will come again and receive you to myself..." and one is left with the faith, the opinion, the guess that: (1) there is a place... (2) that place is going to be better than anything we've seen yet... and (3) we will only understand it when we get there.

One of the last times that I visited Jennifer, we had a great talk about bodies... about the fact that there are better bodies waiting for us. The things Jennifer and I said in that conversation were not really new concepts to either one of us. We had both heard lots of sermons about the life that Christians can look forward to after they shake loose from this earthly existence. The reason that conversation was so meaningful was that Jennifer's body was giving her fits at the moment. Everything was hurting her. Parts that had dependably done their jobs all her life were breaking down... causing pain and frustration. Jennifer's cancer-racked body was giving her hourly messages that it was time for a trade in on a newer model body... a much superior model.

I visited another long-time friend in the hospital as she was dying of cancer. Jude remarked that... as terrible as it was... the pain and the breakdown of bodily processes had a very positive side. I could not imagine what the positive might be until she said, "The whole process helps you separate from your body. It gives you a real clear understanding of what's *you* and what's *your body*... and getting out of that body begins to look like an awfully good idea."

Most of us have become so accustomed to our earthly bodies that we find it nearly impossible to imagine junking the present model with all its problems and moving into a new, imminently superior body to begin our eternal lives. But "planned obsolescence" was not invented by Detroit's automakers. I think God incorporated it into the human body from the first. Scientists estimate that... even with all the best care and conditions... the hinges, muscles, bones, and systems of the body just can't hold together much beyond 120 years. Ask anybody who is approaching half of that 120 years and you will get quick assurance that irreplaceable parts are wearing out fast.

When you think about it, there are many things that we are never going to be able to do or learn as long as we are stuck in these highly limited earthly containers. Whenever you hear or read someone's account of an adventure they call an "out-of-body experience," you are unlikely to hear it described with regret or disgust. The description is almost always one of exhilaration, excitement, pleasure, and freedom. As crazy as we humans are about our bodies... and as much time as we spend preening and pampering them... they do impose upon us lots of restrictions we would love to escape. Stepping out of this earthly body and into the new, improved model that is waiting for us just the other side of death must be the first of many great liberations in store for us.

As Jennifer and her younger sister, Abigail, discussed Abigail's new glasses, Jennifer remarked, "Well, I was supposed to get new glasses too... but I just realized that I won't need them now." I have no trouble picturing Jennifer in her new body... complete with perfect vision and no glasses required. Even before her death, Jennifer's spiritual vision was 20/20.

Do you have any suggestions for God in the design of the bodies to come? I've asked around and had the following features suggested: "No sinuses!" "Unbreakable bones." "Self-flossing teeth." "Toenails that can't become ingrown." "X-ray vision." "The ability to be several places at one time." "Washable brains." "The ability to add or replace memory chips." And "Zippers... to make having babies a lot easier!"

Fortunately, the creator works without such short-sighted input from the creatures. Our vision and our abilities are so limited to this earthly realm that even our best ideas will be simply laughable when the creator finally rolls out the new improved bodies created for our eternal enjoyment.

7

THE MYTH OF
"THE GOOD DEATH"

The famous philosopher, Woody Allen, may have spoken for most people when he commented on death. "It's not that I'm afraid to die," he said, "I just don't want to be there when it happens."

Most of us harbor similar feelings. It's not *death* that we fear... it's *dying*. Dying is something we've never done before. For an event this important, don't we deserve a couple of practice swings beforehand? We rehearse graduations, weddings, and other big events. Why do we have to die with no notice, no rehearsal, no editing, and no chance for "take two?"

After a few childhood tumbles, most of us learn not to work *without a net*. We learn not to get ourselves into situations that are out of our control. In fact, becoming an adult equates roughly to learning grown-up techniques for avoiding pain, indignity, and embarrassing situations. Thereafter, we spend our lives avoiding awkward, compromising predicaments. And then, along comes dying... a process which threatens to involve the whole body in a level of pain we've never sampled before... plus a lot of uncontrollable, embarrassing bodily functions. Dying definitely qualifies as a potentially embarrassing situation... the kind of thing we have learned to avoid at all costs. It is no wonder we are apprehensive about it.

Practically everything we know about dying we learned from television and the movies. Movie makers specialize in "the good death" for characters that the plot has taught us to love and "the payback death" for villains who have had it coming all the way through the story. Here lately, Hollywood has turned gory, undignified, payback dying into a special effects art form... an art form which keeps movie-goers standing in fascinated lines at the box office. We watch those bad guys get theirs in the movies and we wonder, "What if I make a terrible face like that when I am dying? What if I completely lose control and gurgle and scream? What if I bleed and drool like that? I don't want anyone to see me do that. What would people think?"

Yet... even as we put our fears into such words... we begin to see how groundless they are. Hollywood has never been a very trustworthy teacher about the way things really are. We should know better than to base our lives or our fears on versions of reality presented to us by actors, directors, or stunt doubles. But suppose... for the sake of argument... that dying really *does* hurt and you really *do* get messy and sloppy in the process. Why should you care? Why should you worry about the opinion of anybody else who is insensitive enough to care? Humans have been dying for centuries and every single one of them has done it *successfully*. Not all have done it gracefully but... if they made it from alive to dead... their dying was successful.

Dying is the most natural thing in the world. When your time comes, you will do it to perfection. If there is pain, you will respond appropriately to that pain. If there is sickness, your body will react exactly as that sickness causes any body to react. If you make strange sounds or faces, those around you will understand. They may even remark with admiration, "This is not just another social occasion. This person is doing a once-in-a-lifetime thing here... and doing it in a once-in-a-lifetime way."

Because of our uncertainty and apprehension about dying, there has grown up a stereotypical happening which people in the death-and-dying field call "the good death." You know the good death... it's the scene that Hollywood has stored there in the back of your mind. You picture yourself at a ripe old age... propped up comfortably in bed surrounded by adoring family and friends. Beautiful white hair and distinguishing facial wrinkles testify to the fullness of your years. The number of people lovingly gathered around prove the vast number of lives you have touched. One by one, your grateful admirers come forward, hold your hand reverently, and listen as you utter a few simple, but memorable, final words. Then... with every relationship and responsibility perfectly fulfilled... you gaze dramatically off into space, smile with full understanding, and gently close your eyes.

That is "the good death." It is a scene that puts our fears more at ease. If each of us could be sure that we would bring down the curtain on our final act with such an award-winning performance, we might stop digging our fingernails in so deeply to hang onto this life. The writer of the epistle to the Hebrews perfectly described those of us who are afraid of dying. He said in the book's second chapter that Jesus came into the world and conquered death in order to "free those who all their lives were held in slavery by their fear of death."

Whenever some famous authority makes a statement that seems to support the likelihood of the good death, that statement becomes treasured testimony to those of us who are held in slavery by the fear of death. We look for occasions to quote it back and forth to each other. In the early 1900s, a renowned physician named William Osler gave a talk at Harvard in which he said that... of 500 death records he had reviewed... only ninety showed the slightest evidence of pain or distress. It is no wonder that disciples of the good death latched onto the Osler quote and... nearly a century later... continue to keep it shiny with use.

We want all the encouragement we can find. We want the good death to be true... to be probable... to be the exit most likely for us. The myth of the good death calms the fears that we might suffer and gives us hope that we can make a graceful and dignified exit. There are, however, a few problems in our unrealistic anticipation of the good death and our determined pursuit of the Hollywood death-with-dignity scenario.

First, there are the doctors. Modern physicians find it nearly impossible to go against their professional training which is completely oriented toward sustaining life at any cost. Eighty percent of Americans now die behind the sequestered, out-of-sight-out-of-mind walls of hospitals where caregivers are professionally committed to extend life as long as possible... even when it should not be extended at all. Only the most sensitive doctors are beginning to wake up to the rather obvious fact that *quality* of life is what we seek, not a few more weeks of suffering added to our *quantity* of life.

The "STAT team" never fails to make dramatic television as the medical professionals come barreling into the hospital room with hardware and hypodermics to attack the faltering patient and jerk life back into the body. Good television, but a bad way to die. Heroic measures that succeed can give everyone involved a momentary feeling of mastery over death. But heroic measures that fail must certainly constitute the most miserable final experience available for a dying patient. I cannot speak for others, but... when I am heading for life's door anticipating entry into a far superior realm... the last thing I want is an intern barking orders and pounding on my chest.

Hospital staff members follow procedures calculated to keep people alive. If you have executed a living will or a "do not resuscitate" document, make sure you have it posted *prominently* so that nurses and other medical professionals are relieved of their responsibility to jump immediately to routine life-extending procedures. Don't just tell your doctor about your desires. Give the entire staff the benefit of clear communication about your desires regarding final stages.

Our biggest problem in attaining the good death, however, is the lack of cooperation by our own bodies. Physiologically, the systems of the human body do not always shut down with grace and style. No matter what failure of organs or systems brings us to the point of death, we all ultimately die of an inadequate supply of oxygen to the brain. The initial loss of oxygen supply can happen in a way that eases you gently into semi-consciousness or coma and makes you look like one of the lucky ones who drew "the good death." On the other hand, oxygen deprivation can leave you choking, gasping for air, and struggling in a most undignified way.

The physical process of dying can be messy. The body... by simply doing what comes naturally under the conditions... can crush our unfortunate concepts of death with dignity. How tragic that any of us... because of unrealistic expectations of the good death... should actually leave this realm with a last impression that we somehow screwed up dying and failed in the execution of our final earthly act. For patients or their families to hold *style of death* expectations that cannot physically come true is asking for disappointment. We would be much wiser to admit that... regardless of how it happens... the manner in which each of us does death is an inevitable death with dignity. Death is one of a number of life activities that we cannot do wrongly... unless we script impossible scenarios for ourselves.

The question of dealing with the terrible pain of an extended illness is not one with an easy answer. Some experts claim that modern drugs are able to block all pain. Others maintain that some pain remains beyond the numbing power of medication. What do we do when the time comes to die and the pain can't be stopped? Do we endure the pain and its indignities because it is the "hand that we have been dealt?" Or do we voluntarily shorten the process and "die with dignity?"

Each person will make his or her own decision... but advance attention to the various options and possibilities can help us to choose principles by which we want to make our decisions when the time comes. Forethought can also enable us to make legal provisions that will reserve our decision-making rights instead of having them pass to others by default. Though I may change my mind when I actually confront the prospect of severe and irreversible pain, my present attitude... from the naive perspective of the pain-free present... is that I am so committed to the importance of experiencing all that life has to offer... for better or worse... that I intend to play out the whole script until the curtain comes down naturally. I intend to take the pain.

However, I'm not looking for "more than my share" of pain. Should I find myself a terminal patient in a healthcare facility, one of my initial stipulations to those giving me care will be a "Do Not Resuscitate" instruction. What more natural time of departure could there be than when the body loses its own natural power to keep itself going?

Many a traumatic family dilemma over the removal of life support systems could have been avoided if the patient had not been placed on the life support equipment in the first place. When there is no reasonable hope of recovery, there is no reason to resuscitate. I will gladly sign the papers that release the doctors, nurses, and medics from their fear of legal action if they will... when the time comes... bring in the family and then go down to the other end of the hall while I do my dying.

With regard to pain, the word is finally getting around that spending final days in a hospice facility... or under the home care of hospice workers... can completely change the nature of those final days. The hospice movement is not about saving lives but about saving humans from the pain and indignity they usually suffer when care-givers refuse to let them die in peace.

Under hospice care, pain and disease symptoms can be largely removed from the picture. With the terrible side effects of therapy programs out of the way and with pain killers being administered without fear of addiction resulting, the patient can rest easily and focus remaining energies on the important work of departure.

Jennifer's family came to really appreciate the good times that hospice made possible near the end. Jennifer's mother recalls that hospice was especially helpful for the other members of the family: "It was wonderful for all of us to get to be with Jen in the more normal setting of home... to have family devotionals, watch TV, tell her about our days, and to say good-bye. The hospice workers were there to answer all our questions, but Jen could still be in control."

The increasingly popular hospice approach to dying focuses on relieving physical pain and on providing the psychological and social supports needed by patient and family members. Hospice affirms life. It recognizes dying as a normal process. It neither hastens nor postpones death... but involves the patient in decisions about his or her final days... and supports the person in natural progressions toward the end.

To a limited degree, we *can* control the style of our dying by pre-stating our wishes in Living Wills and enforcing those wishes with Durable Powers of Attorney for Healthcare. We can further make the decision to do our dying in our homes or in hospices where we and those we trust maintain some control to the end.

Most importantly, we can use our own minds to avoid the disappointments inherent in the erroneous assumption that... if it's not the good death of the silver screen... it must be a bad death. We can take control of our own expectations and set ourselves up to be more accepting and appreciative of whatever comes. We can take as a role model the boy whose pet mouse fell into a can of varnish and drowned. Someone commented on what a terrible death it must have been and the boy responded, "Maybe... but he sure had a beautiful finish."

8

THE VALUE OF
HUMAN SUFFERING

All the words up to this point about death and the reasons we should not fear it bring up a natural question. "Okay," says a reader. "Suppose I go along with the ideas that death is inevitable... that death is really nothing to fear... that it might even be an event that could be approached with eagerness... and that my awareness of death can actually improve the quality of my life *before* I die. Even if I agree with all that, what am I supposed to do about my fear of the terrible physical torture that I have seen people go through in the process of dying? I hate pain. The final moments of the dying process may be bearable... but what about the weeks, months, even years of agony it sometimes takes to get to those final moments?"

It's a fair question. The beginning of the answer can be found in the weight room at your local health club. Stop by sometime and watch the men and women who are pumping iron. Those people are intentionally making themselves hurt! They are... by deliberate choice and design... causing their various muscle groups to endure significant pain. Some of them even scream and cry out as they do their exercises. Groans. Growls. Grimaces. They are hurting themselves on purpose. And... right there in the middle of all the straining and sweating... you spot the most perfectly developed body in the place. And that body is wearing a T-shirt that proclaims, "No Pain. No Gain."

Body builders know that muscles grow and develop when they are placed under strain. Of course, it has to be the right amount of strain. Overdo it and you can sustain a long-term injury. But use your head as you work those muscle groups and you can carefully take each muscle to its limit and hold it there long enough to intensify its rate of growth and development.

It doesn't require much reflection for us to realize that muscles aren't the only parts of us that develop more intensively under stress... even if that stress crosses the threshold of pain. Think of the proudest achievement of your life. There's a high probability that you endured some discomfort, stress, pain, even suffering to reach that achievement. You went without sleep. You kept working long after you were exhausted. You accepted ridicule from those who thought you were wasting your time. You suffered to reach your goal. What's more... while you would never want to go through it all again... you feel good whenever you remember it.

Suffering is a natural part of life. We avoid it even though it has the potential to make us better. What's the familiar cliché about great artists? We say that they have to suffer before they can truly create. They cannot hope to communicate the heights and depths of human experience until they have visited those extremes.

Most of us react to pain emotionally rather than intellectually. In fact, the struggling we do to resist *anticipated* pain often magnifies the displeasure of the experience and makes it many times worse than it would have been had we not clenched our teeth and tensed our muscles. In medical centers that specialize in the treatment of chronic pain, patients are shown that muscle tension is one of the primary causes of chronic pain. They are taught techniques for monitoring the tensing of muscles, reducing that tension through pain-fighting movements and responses, and strengthening the mind's capacity to disarm and endure discomfort.

Someone might quite honestly say, "Don't talk to me about pain. I can't take it. If it gets too bad, I know how to make it stop. I'll kill myself before I go through that."

A lot of people do. Suicide has been around a long time. Ever since people learned some of the actions by which they could interrupt the body's tendency to continue living and breathing, suicide has been a factor. Some have committed suicide to put an end to pain... either physical suffering or mental anguish. Some have committed suicide as a sort of self-administered capital punishment for shame or social disgrace. Only a statistically insignificant number have committed suicide because they were so enthused about dying that they decided to quit wasting time living.

Interestingly enough, the religious groups that have the most enthusiastic descriptions of the afterlife usually also have the most stringent rules against taking the matter of departure times into your own hands. Many religions have declared suicide an unforgivable sin. They class it as self-murder... as a sinful final act that simultaneously removes all opportunity of asking forgiveness for that final sin. Some religious groups even refuse to conduct funerals for those who have committed suicide. Even in groups that do allow such funerals, the procedures are among the saddest affairs... with mourners trying to say words of comfort to the bereaved without ever mentioning their assumptions about the departed's eternal jeopardy. I don't think these attitudes make much sense.

According to these groups' doctrinal premises, it would seem that they ought to declare equally lost every person who has ever been killed instantly. For... if their doctrine requires that each sin be individually and specifically repented and forgiven prior to death... surely victims of sudden bomb explosions are as likely to enter eternity with unforgiven sins as any suicide victim. Or... if any person is so preoccupied with his or her manner of dying that he or she forgets to utter a last moment request for forgiveness... what eternal hope would remain? The bottom line on the suicide question is that none of us is in any position to make assumptions about any one else's status before their God. If God has the power to forgive sins at all, he certainly can forgive the *socially unacceptable* sin of self-murder as quickly and easily as he can forgive more *socially acceptable* sins like lying, envy, greed, or lust.

Suicide isn't a problem because we discuss and analyze it too much. It continues, spreads, and causes all kinds of long-term guilt for families and friends precisely because we don't talk about it enough. Like death itself, we ought to talk about suicide whenever we think about it. When a teenager is considering it, he or she ought to be able to say, "Listen, loved ones, I feel consummately yucky about everything in general. Suicide is starting to look like a better alternative than life. Any of you ever had thoughts like that? If so, talk to me. Give me some feedback. How come you decided not to do it? How come you're still here?"

Unfortunately, the social stigma of suicide remains with us even in our enlightened age. This often results in an equally great stigma against *talking about* or even *admitting to thoughts of* suicide. And this often results in further isolation of any person considering suicide. And this often results in suicide.

People who commit suicide are rarely the poorest or most desperate... but they *think* they are. Many other people would gladly trade bank accounts and life situations with them...

but, in their depression, suicidal persons cannot imagine why. Movies and television continue to fill us all with unrealistic expectations of life. Our lives continue to fall short of those unrealistic expectations. People we love remain reluctant to discuss the matter. And people... lonely amid crowds... continue to take their own lives.

We learn from suffering. And one of the most valuable things we learn is where *our bodies* end and *we* begin. I visited one man in the hospital who said, "I think what has happened here is that my body has *rejected* me... and I get the feeling that it's going to try and evict me." What valuable new perceptions we gain of ourselves when serious, debilitating, distorting illness tortures the shell in which we are living!

One of the wisest prayer requests I have heard about was from a woman who was visited in the hospital by her minister. When the preacher volunteered to pray for the woman, she suggested, "I want you to pray that I will not *waste* all of this suffering." What wonderful spiritual maturity! Instead of crying out in childish prayer, "Daddy, make it stop hurting!" she was wise enough to pray, "Father, give me the strength and the wisdom I need to plumb the depths of this human experience and learn the lessons that are in it."

Suffering doesn't automatically produce character. In some people it simply produces bitterness. The difference in the result is the material that is under pressure. Hold a ball of clay against a grindstone and it crumbles to dust. Hold an unpolished gem against the same grindstone and you will reveal facets of beauty and strength. But you and I are neither clay nor gemstone. We are humans. And the difference in our material is determined by the mindset with which we choose to meet each trial. We can make a childish response and spend our energy cursing the grindstone and crying out about the unfairness of what has happened to us. Or we can make a mature response and determine to learn from the *opportunity of pain.*

Picture a spoiled child coming to his parent and complaining that every time he rides his bicycle down through the yard he runs into the big oak tree at the turn of the path. What does he want from his parents? Cut down the oak tree of course. "You told me that I should tell you when I needed something," says the kid, "and what I need right now is for you to take that terrible tree out of my way."

The wise parent realizes that the tree is not bad. The child's prayer is simply short-sighted. The child doesn't need the tree moved... he needs to learn to ride the bicycle better. How many of our petitions to our God are those of the spoiled child who once heard in a sermon that God has promised to give us anything we ask? How many of our judgments about what is bad and what is good are simply short-sighted. The longer I live... the more I pray... but the less I tell God how to handle things.

When pain and suffering turn our lives upside down, we cannot always remove the causes... but we can always learn from the experience. In a world where we often fret that we have no time to ourselves, we would do well to turn off the television set in the hospital room, put a "No Visitors" sign on the door if necessary, and make the most of this chance to be alone with our thoughts. While our temporal bodies are making it crystal clear where they end and where our eternal selves begin, we have a wonderful opportunity to inventory the resources with which the real us will be meeting the long-term future.

A time of serious illness or dying can be wonderful or awful... a time to grow or a time to deny. We can talk straight with our loved ones about the things that really matter... or we can beat around the conversational bush, make meaningless small talk, and discuss everything but the obvious... and in so doing... miss golden opportunities and create feelings of guilt that will haunt our survivors until the day they die.

On the other hand, we should not constantly look at death or the sun. There is no positive benefit to be gained by turning a sickroom or a life into a "death zone" where every conversation is so heavy that no one can survive emotionally. We need to honestly discuss our deaths... but only in the realistic context of our lives. There is a wonderful Jewish saying that a person who is dying deserves the respect of being treated like a person who is living. True friends resist the temptation to adopt an artificial, sanitized, condescending conversational style with those who are dying. True friends simply continue the habits of honest conversation and straight talk that would occur if the patient were still well.

There is one way that a visitor to a sickroom may discuss the weather, the news, and lighthearted topics for the purpose of denying the reality of a sickness. There is another way in which a true friend can discuss those same topics simply because they are the makings of normal conversation... even if the person being visited is unquestionably terminal. The unspoken message of the true friend's conversation is, "Just because you are dying doesn't mean that your interest in life... or my honesty with you... has disappeared. Our friendship transcends life and death. Because of our unique relationship, you and I can discuss the weather in one breath and death in the next. We are beyond any requirement for formally prepared communiques."

Perhaps the toughest part of human suffering is not the part the sick person does. It is the infuriating frustration that must be endured by those who helplessly stand by and watch the pain. In the same way, dying may be a snap for the person who is ready to do it... but pure torture for those who have to do the letting go. Neither relief at the cessation of pain nor faith in eternal life can eliminate the natural grief and pain of human separation. Believing that you and I will meet again does not stop me from missing you desperately when you first leave me. And... even after the missing reduces itself to a dull ache... it will remain with me. The pain of letting go will never completely leave me. Like the contamination of nuclear fallout, it will merely reduce itself by half-lives until I have drawn my last breath.

But... if the physical pain of sickness and dying are major learning opportunities of life... so too is the sword through the heart that we call grief. Given all my formal education and all my life experiences, no event ever taught me more than the enduring pain of grief over three boys who died on a cold December evening.

9

YOU HAVE TO DIE TO REALLY LIVE

I woke up knowing I had cancer. It was a Saturday morning. The whole family was sleeping late. I lay there enjoying warm pillows and soft sheets. But... as my hand touched my side... I felt a bump under the skin that I had never felt before. "That's it!" I thought. "Here I am thirty years old... with a wife and three kids... just bought a house in a new city... started a new job... and I've got cancer. I'm going to die."

I lay there and thought about dying. I felt surprisingly calm. No panic. No regrets. "Thirty years old," I thought. "Not the time I would have picked to exit the scene but I'm sure that... if I were seventy... I would still have had a long list of things I wanted to do. Considering the length of eternity, what difference would another forty years make anyway? Dying now just means that somebody else will have to paint the gutters on this house."

I got out of bed, took a shower, and dressed to visit a doctor whom I knew had Saturday morning office hours. My thoughts... from my bed to the doctor's office door... were different from my thoughts on any previous Saturday morning. I saw things along the way that I had never seen before. I saw familiar sites with brand new eyes. From colors of flowers to the frustrations of traffic, I was looking at everything with a simultaneous first and last glance. I looked at things more *carefully* than ever before... because I doubted I would have many more chances to look at them again.

I don't recall a time when my mind was more alert to my surroundings. If I ever had a set of senses custom-tailored to "stop and smell the roses" it was on that Saturday morning. As Samuel Johnson is famous for saying: "The prospect of death wonderfully concentrates the mind."

You have probably figured out how the story ends... or maybe you have lived it yourself. The doctor checked the bump on my side and said, "It's nothing... just a bump under your skin. Nothing to worry about."

I drove back home feeling relieved. The terminal condition which had been absolutely real to me an hour earlier was now just a bump under the skin. But... in addition to my relief... I could not help being amazed at the difference my awareness of "death" had made in my way of looking at everything. I was equally amazed at all the things I no longer worried about while I thought I was about to die. There was the mortgage I would not have to pay. There were problems I would not have to solve. Even my concerns about the well-being of Kay and the kids were minimal. "I'll miss them... and they'll miss me... but somehow a future will be worked out."

The saddest part of this story is that I am unable to report honestly that the colors of the flowers were as vibrant on the drive home as they were on the drive to the doctor's office. I wish I could say that my life and values *after* my "Saturday morning cancer" were as clarified and certain as they were *during* the episode. They weren't. Life crowded back in, overwhelmed me with details, and convinced me that a lot of things were critically important that in truth were not very important at all.

As subsequent brushes with death occurred... and then as Kay and Rick and I struggled to survive the sudden deaths of Tim and Don and Bryan... death became less of a fleeting experience and more of an awareness that came to stay. I see things today through eyes that cannot forget the likelihood of death. And... while I do feel richer for this perception... I also realize that it is not a license to be a crepe-hanging party pooper at every opportunity. I try to remind myself often of the old codger some friends told me about. These friends were showing off their beautiful new baby girl at church. The crotchety old brother took one look at the infant and remarked, "Well, she's gonna be a beautiful child... if she lives."

Death awareness is accumulated wisdom to help us with life's events. It is not a wet blanket for continuous discouragement of others. The paradox is that our most treasured relationships and possessions can only be truly appreciated after we have dealt with the reality of their eventual loss. The true values of life become momentarily clear as we consider them through the objective eyes of a person who is about to leave them behind. No one is more evangelistic about the ways life should be lived than the person who has just returned from a "near death experience." These voyagers have had a clear and undistorted look at what is truly valuable and what is not.

Death is a whole new way of looking at life. It recalls to our thinking the beneficial pilgrim concept held by so many of the early American colonists. Their religious beliefs stressed that they were just "wayfaring strangers wandering through this world of woe." Whether their situation was terrible or wonderful, it was only temporary. Those pilgrims were able to cope with hardship because they were convinced of the transience of life's blessings and problems. Their real home was yet to be reached. They were only passing through.

For any of us to think of ourselves as permanent residents of this life is to maintain a relation to the world that is built on an illusion. If you believe that your existence will continue on the other side of death, then the most intimate relationships of your life... bonds with father and mother, with brothers and sisters, with spouses and children, with communities, and nations... all become less important than your relationship to the one who holds eternity. No aspect of your earthly life can ignore the permanence of God and the impermanence of earthly life. And it is no sacrifice to give up that which you cannot keep in order to gain that which you cannot lose.

But... even if you believe that there is no eternity... you still must live your life and make your choices with full awareness of your impending death. The things you value, the priorities you set, the way you spend each golden moment all have to agree with your strongly held conviction that "when it's over, it's over." With no anticipation of life beyond the grave, your logical goal is to reach the final moment of your life with no regrets about the ways you spent all your previous moments.

The Muslims have an impressive practice in connection with the pilgrimage to Mecca that every Muslim male is supposed to make once in a lifetime. The pilgrims always stop some distance from Mecca to wash, pray, and change into a special gown called an *ihram*. If they are traveling by plane, pilgrims change into the *ihram* before the plane touches down at Mecca. The *ihram* consists of two pieces of unsewn white cloth. It is worn throughout the visit to Mecca. Its purpose is to remind the pilgrim hour after hour that he is prepared to give up everything for God. It is also a reminder to every pilgrim that... when he or she dies... every earthly possession will become meaningless. It is a valuable thought for Muslim or non-Muslim to recall every day that we live.

Regardless of our assumptions about life beyond the grave, the deceptions by which material things dominate our lives is amazing. We know that things cannot satisfy us... and yet we continue to fall for their promises of happiness. We know from experience that... however much we have... it will always be a little less than we want... and yet we keep falling for the myth that a little more will secure our happiness.

I had a friend in high school whose only wish in life was to save enough money to buy a new guitar which was priced at $26 in the music department at Sears. He eventually got the guitar, learned to play it, and actually succeeded as a professional song writer. He wrote "Little Green Apples," "Honey," "That's the Night the Lights Went Out in Georgia," and other hits. I went to visit him once in Los Angeles after he had hit the big time. His new hobby was owning race horses. He was trying hard to write another big hit song because there was a particular race horse he wanted to buy. The price of that horse was $26,000. I couldn't help but note how life keeps adding zeroes to stay ahead of our desires. A $26 guitar or a $26,000 race horse. There's no catching up with our desires for the things of this world.

There is nothing inherently wrong with owning guitars or race horses. Our problem occurs when the things we want... come to own us. A constant awareness of death can alert us to the true values of the things we crave. It can give us a perception of reality that enables us to own things without being enslaved by them. Without this enlightenment, we are forever in danger of confusing earthly life with real life... of confusing the rehearsal with the real show.

If this life is all there is, then it is doubly important to carefully spend our energy getting only those things that are worth what they cost us... and wasting none of our precious time or energy chasing useless possessions. If our thinking makes us anticipate a life beyond the grave, our relationship with the world's material goods shifts into an entirely different gear.

Only those who maintain their awareness of the inevitable have the power to reject the overwhelming appeal of this world's glittering tangibles. For those who anticipate no life beyond the grave, awareness of the inevitable is necessary to avoid wasting precious time and energy on a treadmill of getting and spending. On the other hand, a constant awareness of inevitable death is equally important to those who believe their lives will never end. They must make their time and energy decisions in favor of values and relationships that can outlast earthly life.

Unfortunately, not many of us are smart enough on our own to identify and remember to seek first the things that really matter. In my experience, it has been close brushes with death that have turned on the light... that have made it suddenly clear to me which things can last and which ones are fleeting. In the process of grappling with death's mystery, we begin to understand life's secret.

In a very real sense, we cannot really live until we die. It is by overcoming the fear of losing that we gain the emotional security required to take life's big risks. Confidence is being able to say to ourselves, "Well, the worst that could happen to me in this is that I die... and that's not such a big deal." The most successful sales person in any company is the one who has lost his or her fear of falling short of the quota and has become immersed in serving customers. The best player on any athletic team is the one who is so busy striving for perfection that there is no thought of simply "playing not to lose."

Only after we come to the full realization that we are going to die (and maybe soon) are we able to take life in hand and allow it to work *for* us instead of *against* us. Jesus spoke about the "truth setting us free" and it is a certainty that the truth about life and death has the ability to set us free from the bondage of life, its false promises of security, and its alluring but unsatisfying goodies.

Christianity's sudden and unprecedented spread around the Roman world has often been attributed to the fact that the early believers were suddenly able to see life and death through entirely new eyes. Suddenly, they were not afraid to die! The pagan world was intrigued by such unnatural courage in the face of threatened death. It was common knowledge that all people had their breaking points. You could ultimately make people bend to your will if you threatened them with death. Normal people could be expected to do anything to save their skins.

But these Christians were different. They were not afraid to die. Indeed, some of them even thanked their executioners for hastening their departures to a better existence. They went to tortuous deaths with confident songs on their lips. The pagans could not fathom such power over life's ultimate threat. They demanded to know the secret. The Christians gladly told them the secret. And Christianity spread through the Roman world like wildfire.

It is our philosophies of death that will enable us to live decently and die well. A philosophy that all things end at the grave should enable us to live without hesitancy... love without reservation... face death without regret... bury our loved ones and move ahead without looking back. On the other hand, a philosophy that life extends beyond the grave makes possible victorious life even in the face of apparent life tragedies. People who have learned the lessons death has to teach can start life all over again with a brand new set of rules... a set of rules that enhances the quality of their lives.

10

EAT THE DESSERT FIRST

I've seen the sign many places since... but I still remember the first time I saw it. Kay and I had rented a car and were wandering through miles and miles of South Dakota. It was only a couple of years after the boys had died and we were enjoying the beauty and solitude of uninterrupted prairies and grasslands. Eventually, we rolled into a small town and stopped to eat at the local cafe. We slid into the only booth that wasn't filled with real cowboys and cowgirls. There on the wall of the booth was a little card that said, "Life is short. Eat the dessert first."

We didn't... eat the dessert first... but we did love the sentiment of the card. Our accumulation of life experiences had already made us strong believers in doing once-in-a-life-time things as soon as possible. I had watched too many people of my own age sacrifice their lives to the American dream sequence: "once we get the kids through school, pay off the mortgage, and retire, we are going to do what we've always wanted to do."

Though we have never fit the mold of hippie hitch-hik-ers, Kay and I have shared from the first a sentiment that... if we could possibly find the ways and means... death was not going to sneak up on us and catch us saying, "if only we had..." Through the years, we've exchanged our chances to have matching furniture, fashionable wardrobes, and corpo-rate careers for chances to go some places and do some things that others only dream about.

The lessons of death can make you stop "putting off until later" things that you really need to go ahead and do today. In fact, it would not be hard to make a case that sudden aware-ness of impending death lies behind the stereotypical "mid-life crisis" that so often turns conservative CPAs into drivers of flamboyant little sports cars. The sudden realization that "not only am I going to die... but I am over half-way there..." is enough to turn the most reserved of us a little "middle aged crazy."

The first full-time job I ever had was as an underpaid school teacher in rural southern Georgia. Kay and I struggled through that first year and even added our first-born to our family on less annual salary than it now costs just to have a baby. But the good news hit us just as school finally ended for the year. We discovered that... though the nine-month school year was now completed... we were receiving our sal-ary on a twelve-month schedule. Inadequate as it was, our monthly salary was going to continue all summer long.

We were living in a dump, had a baby only a few months old, and had plenty of reasons that I should get a summer job and get us a little ahead financially. But the idea hit us that we had a perfect opportunity to see the U.S.A... even if we had to travel on a shoe string. We discovered that our double bed mattress would fit neatly inside our Volkswagen bus with just enough room left for Rick's porta-crib behind it. We made some screens and curtains for the windows... stashed a camp stove and boxes of groceries on the floor under the mattress...

got a road map and plotted a route from Georgia to California that connected all the places where we had relatives or college friends... and headed west.

This happened long enough ago that it was neither illegal nor unsafe to sleep overnight in roadside parks... so we only had to pay for lodging one night... a whopping $1.50 to park in a campground outside Carlsbad Caverns. Rick learned to crawl on that double bed mattress with picture windows all around him providing views of the Painted Desert, the Grand Canyon, and Boulder Dam. We even stayed with acquaintances in Los Angeles who were good friends of Pat and Shirley Boone and topped off our LA visit with a dip in the Boone's swimming pool.

We had plenty of trying times and more than a few discomforts on what has come to be known as "the year we camped to California" but we have never had the first regret that we made the trip. If we had stayed in south Georgia and I had gotten a summer job, we would have made a little extra money... and we would have spent a little extra money. But we would never have had the "year we camped to California." We ate the dessert first that summer and we have enjoyed the memories of it every year since.

A few years later, we had a chance to go and live in New Zealand for a while. It was totally inconvenient and completely out of step with couples our age who were buying and furnishing nice homes and building corporate careers. We reduced our collection of stuff to one large shipping crate and took off to New Zealand as Charlie, Kay, Rick, and Tim. Three years later, we returned as Charlie, Kay, Rick, Tim, *and Don*. We made lots of sacrifices to experience New Zealand... but we have friends and memories there that are worth more to us than new houses and corporate careers. We ate the dessert first... and we are so glad we did.

The same thing happened when I made the move to freelance writing. I had been moonlighting, writing scripts and brochures and textbooks at night to make ends meet. The first year that I made as much from moonlighting as I made from my regular job, I began to think I might be able to make it as a free-lance writer. I never expected that I would make *more* money. I just wanted to make as much and have more time at home with "our three knuckleheads" who were growing up fast. It was a risk. It did not happen without rough spots. But working at home did give me a lot more time with Kay and the boys. In retrospect, I am so glad that I took the time *then* since... with Tim and Don... there wasn't going to be any later.

Without a doubt, the biggest serving of dessert that we ever ordered for ourselves was our family trip to Europe. As the boys were on the brink of their teenage years... and the free-lancing had been going pretty well... it occurred to us that we would never have a better chance to make a family tour of Europe. We carved five weeks out of the summer calendar... bought five plane tickets and five Eurail passes... found somebody to house sit for free... packed one bag for each of us... and went to Europe.

The book I wrote about our trip was called *Europe Without Reservations* and that is exactly how we traveled. We would start out each morning with absolutely no idea where we would be sleeping that night. We saw parts of England, France, Belgium, Holland, Germany, Austria, Switzerland, Italy, and Spain that most tourists never have a chance to see. We walked and wandered and stumbled and fumbled through big cities and small villages. We stayed with friends of friends with whom we still correspond... people who have been to visit in our home many times since.

We never failed to find a bed for the night though some nights it was chancy and some nights it was only two beds for the five of us. We saw the sights, rode the subways, stayed lost a lot of the time, ate in the bistros, had my pocket picked in Rome, and lost Don for around two hours in a town where no one spoke English. By the time our five weeks were up, we had all had plenty of Europe and plenty of each other. But... in the years since... the stories and memories have become priceless.

My recollection is that we made the whole trip for about $5,000. Just think of all the things we could have bought with $5,000! Things for the house. A newer car. College savings for the boys. Lots of things. But that trip to Europe was the best $5,000 we ever spent. It bought memories that can never be replaced. We could not take that trip now for any amount of money... since the original cast of characters is no longer together.

The point of this chapter is not to tell you about places our family has gone and things we've done... though I must admit I enjoyed going through the memories one more time. The point is that there is some trip that you need to stop putting off and go ahead and take. Or maybe you've been putting off getting serious about your hobby... or learning another language... or going back to school... or walking the Appalachian Trail... or bungee jumping... or arranging a way to meet personally someone whom you have admired from afar for many years.

Whatever it is, *eat your dessert now*. It will never be cheaper and... if you keep putting it off... you could miss the chance to do it at all. Don't risk finding yourself staring up at the ceiling of an ambulance as it hurries you through traffic to the Coronary Care Unit while your mind keeps repeating, "Here I am about to die and I never took that whitewater rafting trip down the Colorado."

Of course, not every dream is an expensive one. One man faced his heart attack and realized that... even though he was a successful business executive... he had never taken the time to buy the hunting rifle that he had been promising himself for so many years. Another time, a group of friends sat around after dinner talking about things they had always wanted to do. Most of them had dreams with extremely high price tags attached to them. But one man said that he had achieved almost everything he ever wanted except to own a $100 box of fine cigars. The friends talked it over, chipped in the money on the spot, and thoroughly enjoyed watching him light up and fulfill a lifetime dream in their presence.

Money is not usually the problem. Most of us can find ways financially to do things that we consider essential. But doing the thing that you've always wanted to do is rarely convenient. You have to decide to do it and then tenaciously work out the details until there is nothing left to stop you. The ingredient that most of us lack is the incentive to do it *now* because now is all we have. There is a familiar line that no man on his death bed ever said, "I really wish I had spent more time at the office."

Life is short. Eat the dessert first. The alternative is to keep living in the same rut and dreaming about the things you *would* do if you won the lottery. There is almost a statistical certainty that you are not going to win the lottery. On the other hand, your probability of death is quite a different statistical story.

Recognizing that life is short will also effect the way you go about eating the dessert. Be sure you *eat* the dessert... instead of just taking a roll of photos of it... or shooting five minutes of home video of the dessert with your spouse standing in front of it. I have nothing against photographs and the memories they can bring back... but I have taken a few trips where I stayed so busy capturing the experience on film for later home viewing that I failed to soak up the full experience of actually being there. Don't be like the man who returned to work and, when asked whether he had a good vacation, replied, "I don't know... I haven't gotten the pictures developed yet."

In conclusion... just a tiny disclaimer. Eat the dessert first but don't bite off more than you can chew. If you wanted to be a bull fighter in your younger years, don't jump into a ring with El Toro when you are age 67. Remember to consider your significant others in your plan—it's no good to sell the family home and buy a boat to sail the South Seas if you are the only one in the family who enjoys the water. And don't mortgage your future just to be able to say you ate the dessert. Use your head. Be systematic. Almost as good as *doing* the thing you've always wanted to do is setting a date for doing it and working your way through the steps required to do it. All of us are going to die with some unfinished plans. The real tragedy though is to die without even making a plan.

Take as your goal... arrival at your moment of death able to say to yourself, "Life has been great. I've done my thing. Now, let's see what this death thing is all about."

11

NO UNFINISHED BUSINESS

One office worker gained a reputation among his colleagues for interrupting his assignments to do other things on the spur of the moment. In the middle of a task, he might look out the window and see an old person who needed help crossing the street. Whatever he was doing went on hold until the old person had been helped. His assignments *did* eventually get done... but not before he stopped to make a baby laugh or help a delivery man with a parcel. When someone finally asked him about his low resistance to interruptions, he explained, "When I was in Vietnam, my job was to clear minefields. I always knew that my next step might be my last. So, I learned to tend to all important business *before the next step*. Land mines would wait... but the one thing I didn't want was to be blown sky high thinking about something I had put off that I really wanted to do."

Professionals who work with terminal patients say that the ones who are most troubled... who have the hardest time with the prospect of dying... are those who still have "unfinished business." They are the patients who are still carrying grudges or guilt or old scores that need to be settled before they can gain the emotional closure required for peace of mind. As one old codger finally admitted, "I've still got somebody I want to cuss out."

Whether it's a cussing out or the request for forgiveness that would probably follow that cussing out, we have to finish our unfinished business if we hope to die well... or to live well. The old saying that warns us not to "let the sun go down on our wrath" is warning us about unfinished business. Each of us has the ability to lighten the emotional load that we will carry to death's door. We can take the steps required to resolve minor conflicts before they grow into long-standing vendettas. We can swallow our embarrassment and heal broken relationships when they happen... instead of years later. We can express appreciations when they first occur to us... instead of procrastinating until it is too late.

It almost seems as if some humans *treasure* their unfinished business until it is too late to deal with it. Most of us have met people who relish the fact that they have not spoken to a friend or relative in years. You get the feeling that they would rather tell you the long story of how they were wronged than never to have been wronged at all. Unfinished business has a certain appeal to it. It adds a little soap opera excitement to our lives. But it loses its appeal at the moment we realize there is no time left to clear up the feud. Some people seem to enjoy living in a nest of smoldering relationships. They assume that they will clean up the clutter at the last minute. But death often arrives unannounced... or... removes our strength for problem-solving as it commences. Those who run out of last minutes when they still have a lot of last-minute business are understandably troubled as they face death.

On the other hand, people who have cleared the slate, paid the bills, canceled their subscriptions, and stopped buying green bananas tend to say "Okay, Death... Let's see what you've got." One confident and totally prepared man was reported to have departed this life with the words, "Now, *this* should be interesting!"

Most people like the *idea* of living with all unfinished business up to date... but they soon realize that it is much more easily described than accomplished. For most, "living up to date" requires a change of values and life style. Almost no one can commit to "living ready" and immediately be that way. There is a period of hard work that lies between most of us and being ready to go. We may need months to retrain ourselves financially... to take control of our bill-paying habits to the degree that we are finally able to dispatch bills as they arrive rather than agonizing over which bills will get paid when there is too much month at the end of the money.

Most people need to start by spending some hours organizing the paperwork of their lives... putting wills and deeds and important contact information into forms where even a stranger can find things. People who are organized and efficient in their jobs often claim to be unable to "get organized" in their personal lives. Ask to see the important papers in some families and you are in for a hilarious journey through the contents of a bottomless kitchen drawer or other household stash. Ask to see the deed to the house or the rent agreement and you get to follow your leader through a catch-all that contains the household hammer, the kids' first artwork, a half-melted candle, old recipes, expired coupons, and some of the most important papers the family will ever have to search for.

The peace of mind that can result from having things organized is not just a benefit to those taking their last breaths. It is a benefit to those in the busiest moments of daily life. Having the details of your life in order is something that *can* be accomplished and *can* remove a vast quantity of those out-of-focus items that swirl around in cluttered minds. Tend to it... get it organized... and drop it from your list of worries.

You don't have to be an efficiency expert or a computer whiz to get organized. The simplest materials can give your life a feeling of mastery and control. A few file folders... a loose-leaf notebook with dividers... boxes with labels... whatever system works for you. The most important thing in choosing an organizational system is to remember that... when that system is called upon to really do its thing... *you will not be present to explain how the system works.* You will not be standing there to say, "You may think this is kind of weird but you'll find all the information about our car payments in the pocket of my old jacket in the hall closet."

Give your loved ones a break! Don't let your important papers become a household treasure hunt. Put them into some system that any literate person can understand. Instead of the pocket of your old jacket... where things will eventually be discovered five years too late... give your survivors the blessing of a household file drawer. Fill it with file folders labeled "Car, Payments" and "Car, Maintenance Records." Organization is not a difficult thing to accomplish... but it is one that will be appreciated by your grieving loved ones.

"Living ready" does not mean that we get everything organized and then stop living. On the contrary, it means that... however long we happen to live after we get organized for departure... we can live with a lot less confusion, a lot fewer things lost, and a lot less time wasted in unnecessary hand-wringing and searching. "A place for everything and everything in its place." You've heard it all your life. You already do it in some parts of your life. Is it too much to ask that you do it in the parts of your life that your loved ones will have to clean up after you have left the scene?

While organizing the paperwork of your life is relatively simple, there is a tougher... but equally important... set of unfinished business to take care of. The chain of human relationships that have made up your life may be tangled and knotted but the time for straightening out that business is now...

rather than later or not at all. A good friend told me about his awkward feelings when he decided to make a special visit to his grandparents to tell them how much he appreciated all they had done for him through the years. It wasn't a holiday visit. It wasn't a visit because someone was sick. There was no *social excuse* for the visit. He simply wanted to say thank you. His grandparents were deeply touched. The resulting conversation had a richness that might never have occurred otherwise. My friend reached a new relationship with two people who are very important to him. Equally important, his frequent thoughts of his grandparents are no longer plagued by second thoughts about unfinished business.

When you have shared enough of a friend's life to be the one who can best help in that friend's death, skip the small talk by which you both pretend that earthly existence is not coming to an end. Talk about things that have mattered to both of you. Let the natural conversation reveal things that your friend may want or need to do... friends he or she may want to see... places that need visiting one last time... life business that needs to be settled. Of course, you will have to make allowances for physical or emotional limitations imposed by your friend's condition but... to whatever extent you can help... *you* have unfinished business as long as your friend does. You don't want to lie on your own death bed and think to yourself, "I could have made Harry's last wish come true. If I had taken a day off from work, I could have helped Harry finish that piece of business." Take the day off. Make up the time later. Deal with unfinished business. It will enrich Harry's death and your life.

In the early days of Christianity, there was a tradition of forgiving everyone from the death bed. Family members and other associates were gathered around the person who was dying. In a brief conversation with each, the person forgave them for anything they might have done to him or her. No doubt, the dying person also asked forgiveness of each visitor. And almost certainly they recalled together the pleasant memories they shared. It was a wonderful moment of closure and completeness for each. No denial that death was at the door. No embarrassment over tears of separation. Just honest, undistorted, loving communication to conclude a valued relationship.

People who know they are dying can be great conversationalists. They don't have time to play games. They will tell you the truth... once you make it clear that you can handle the truth. Their directness is such a refreshing change from the elusive conversational sleight of hand we see so often in daily life. What a tremendous enrichment of your life and mine... if we could incorporate the deathbed perspective so fully into our thinking that our daily communications would be honest and direct. To say the least... it would take some getting used to!

Jennifer was a great example of patience and total honesty about the cancer that was taking her life. Even after chemotherapy had stolen her hair, she chose to go without a wig. One day in a store, Jennifer and her mother were confronted by a little old lady who was obviously unaware of the effects of chemotherapy. "What happened to him?" the little lady asked. While Jennifer's mom was still trying to decide how best to answer, Jennifer responded calmly, "I have bone cancer." "Well, why did you shave your head?" the lady inquired. Jennifer patiently explained the process of chemotherapy and how it usually causes the hair to fall out. In that brief conversation, Jennifer educated... encouraged... forgave... and skipped over an opportunity to be cruel and vindictive and "put the woman in her place." Jennifer's awareness of death made clear to her the absolute uselessness of a cutting response... and the absolute value of that little old lady.

Later in her journey, Jennifer's strong belief in life after death resulted in an inspirational and much-repeated incident. When it became obvious that the first year of chemotherapy had not stopped her cancer, the doctors gathered around Jennifer's bed and offered her the option of an additional course of experimental chemotherapy. After a full year of chemo and the amputation of her right leg, Jennifer's immediate response was, "No. I'm ready to go to heaven." That was her answer. Straightforward and clear. Disarmingly honest. And I am told that a nurse standing nearby said in all sincerity, "May I go with you?"

If you have not taken the opportunity to visit your acquaintances who have terminal conditions, I encourage you to do so. They are our greatest living experts on dying. They are struggling through uncharted territory and... if my experience is typical... they would love to share that experience with you. One of the most common complaints of terminally ill patients is that you and I don't come to see them... don't take the opportunity to walk a while with them in the valley of the shadow of death.

Of course, they *are* sick. And there are times when they can't or don't want to share time with anybody. There are some days when they are too considerate to subject you to their nausea and unrelenting pain. But other times... they love the fact that you want to visit. They know that many other activities are demanding your presence. But the medium is the message... you are *there*. You came to talk. More important, you came to listen. You are not afraid to touch them and treat them as if they are still living... which they most certainly are. Even when they progress beyond conversation... when they are comatose or highly sedated... they still hear you... they still feel your touch... and they still know that you are there... treating them honestly like a person who is both living and dying... as we all are.

The blessing of the terminally ill is that they are less and less distracted by the things that don't really matter. Unlike those of us who overlook our terminal characteristics, they are not wasting their limited time and energy on life's material goods and trivial busy-ness. The time we spend with those who are dying reminds us of the importance of applying the "ten year test" to the issues of our lives. Instead of allowing ourselves to be tied in knots by life's requirements and demands, we must learn to ask ourselves, "How important will this be ten years from now?" Many of the things that worry us are placed in their proper perspectives by application of the ten year test. And... for even greater perspective... try the "hundred year test."

Besides its importance in the days of dying, unfinished business is an equally valuable way of looking at the days of living. We need to see the frenzied activities of our lives more as the kids in playschool perceive the activities of their days. Whether you are getting out a critical report at the office or building an important tunnel in the playschool sandbox, you do it for all you are worth... yet never forget as you do it that the project will not pass the ten year test. Whether you are building a skyscraper of concrete and steel or a tower of blocks on the kitchen floor, you do it the best you can... but never forget that *you* are more permanent than either kind of building. It is my guess that... when time has ceased and skyscrapers have lost their usefulness... your spirit will still exist. The invisible spirits of your friends and acquaintances... and your relationships with those spirits... are far more important and lasting than any of the tangibles of your life will ever be.

Even if it were my conviction that everything would cease at the grave, I hope that conviction would keep me from trading my life too cheaply. I have nothing but time... and an undetermined amount of that. I must never trade my irreplaceable minutes for activities or experiences of low value. Only one life... I must make it count.

The moral of unfinished business is not that we cannot be involved in anything that we cannot complete at one sitting. There are many things that we need to do that require lengthy time investments. Having no unfinished business does not mean that we must finish every task by the end of the day. But there *is* a special peace of mind in leaving your work bench knowing that you have left your project at a "good stopping place." As I work on the manuscript of this book, I am constantly aware that... if I die before I have completed the final chapter... the notes and ideas for the remaining chapters are already down on paper. Someone else can take this project up and carry it to completion. This book contains concepts that I have learned the hard way and I want to know that they will be available to others. But... if I walk away from my word processor tonight and die before I ever get back to this keyboard... I will know that I have done what I could and that I left the project at a "good stopping place."

"Living caught up" saves us from a frenzied rush to get everything done at the last minute. If I should receive word today that I will die at this time tomorrow, I will give Kay and Rick extra long hugs, make a few brief phone calls, and probably put in my usual time here at the keyboard.

The lesson of ever-imminent death is very "deliberate living." Because we are aware of the certain end to our lives, we determine to experience and celebrate each stage of life as it occurs. Our awareness of death gives us the power to look beyond pain and even recognize long-term values of painful and unpleasant events of life. And... because we have developed the habit of *living* deliberately and responsibly... we can confront our *deaths* the same way. Whether the end of your life occurs suddenly aboard an airliner spinning out of control into the earth or through some long-and-drawn-out illness, you can die deliberately... knowing that you have tended to all the unfinished business... kept your good-byes constantly up to date... and are ready for the next adventure. You can look squarely at the final moments of your earthly life and say, "Now... *this* should be interesting!"

12

PLANNING FOR YOUR DEATH

I made it this far in this book before I remembered that our youngest son, Don, had written his own will before he died in a freak accident at the age of nineteen. Don had just graduated from high school and knew he wanted some kind of a change before even thinking about college. A family we knew was getting ready to move to the mountains of eastern Honduras to start a medical clinic. Don asked if he could go along and help. They said yes and Don had about a month to get ready.

After Don had left for Honduras, we found a large brown envelope on his bed. His class ring was sitting on top of the envelope which contained a collection of snapshots of Don through the years and several sheets of notebook paper in Don's unmistakable printing style. He had decided that capital letters cramped his creativity so he was doing all his printing in lower case letters. As I typed a few passages from Don's will into this chapter, my word processing software objected constantly because it is programmed to automatically capitalize the first word in every sentence. Don would have been pleased.

> *i, donald w. walton, being of existing mind and underweight body, do hereby declare the following to be my last will and testament and though i never dictated it to a lawyer, give a dead man a break from all that legal stuff for once, huh?*

> *mom and dad. i never really thanked you for the upbringing job you did on me. all in all, i think you did a pretty decent job. i thank you whole-heartedly for always being there to help me financially or any other way you could. i appreciated your helping words without coddling. you're the best parents I ever had and the only ones I would ask for the second time around. my thanks and my love remain with you. i declare all my worldly possessions be left to you (with the following exceptions) to be sold, given to charity, or donated to the donald w. walton memorial museum. whatever you see fit.*

> *to my best friend, bryan, i leave all the memories of all the many times we've shared together. go ahead and write the bron book and make it a best seller. i wish i had something of real value to give to you, but you'll have to settle for this. you know how much i love music. i want you to have all the records and tapes in my personal collection (except for led zeppelin's fourth album and houses of the holy album, which are on one tape). i hope as you listen to any of this music, you'll think of me—cause you can bet i'll be somewhere banging out "stairway to heaven" on a harp. i love you, friend. so long. be happy. and when you get to heaven, look me up.*

to warren. i give back to you the guitar you gave to me. you also know of my love for music. i will that, though you couldn't save me, you will never let our music die. if i have the right, i leave you the rights to any and all the music we ever wrote together. i also leave you the rights to any of my own lyrics. record a top-ten album and dedicate it to me (because i've always wanted to have an album dedicated to me). thanks for all the times we've shared. take care of yourself, big guy, and carry on.

to the federal government of the united states of america, i leave any and all unpaid debts (public and private) that i may have accumulated up until the point of my death. pay them in full, in good health, and without an unkind word or gripe, for it is my last will.

to medical science, i give any part of my physical body that may be needed for either research or transplant. i pray it works better for you than it did for me.

i will that my funeral consist of a closed-casket ceremony. accompanying this final document are a few pictures of me that I was able to scratch up. i would like these (and any other photos that you see appropriate) to be displayed in chronological order atop my coffin. i would like for the photographs to be accompanied by the legend:

> *"do not remember don as he is now... for he isn't. rather, remember him as you knew him."*

i would like also to ask that bright-colored clothing replace the traditional mourning attire. anything that has to be done to keep the service from being dreary should be done. i ask that the song "one more arrow" by elton john be played. there should be music, laughter, happiness, and rejoicing for i've moved on to a much happier place. i ask that my tombstone carry the epitaph:

> *"do not spend much time at this place of burial... don didn't."*

to tim, i leave a last request. i would like for you to hold a "come as your favorite dead person" party in my honor. however, no one is to dress as me. if i don't show up, then credit my absence to the fact that i've moved and left no forwarding address. hold the party anywhere you like but hold it on the same date every year until everyone loses interest and decides not to show. if anyone tells you that to hold a "come as your favorite dead person" party in my honor is tacky, simply tell them to go soak their head someplace. we need no skeptics around when we're trying to party.

to julie, brian, michael, jennifer, ellen, laurel, scott, tavin, and warren, i will you all to remember the 4th of july party at the yellow river. it was unanimous with us to make the event a tradition. please carry on the tradition. shoot off fireworks. laugh. cry. hug each other. smoke cigars. go to the waffle house and eat bacon and hash browns. and hey, shoot off a bottle rocket for me, huh? i love you guys.

and finally... to the most important person ever to cross the path of my life. you made me laugh and cry. but most of all, you made me cherish life. i had never feared death. i was always ready to accept it. i never really cared if I lived or died... until I met you. it was then that I had second thoughts of dying. second thoughts not because of ceasing to live, but ceasing to be able to spend time with you for you made my life worthwhile. i leave with you the memories of all the times we spent together. i give you every dream song that has ever been written, as well as every dream that i have ever dreamed. i thank you for loving me, treating me as no one else would (or could) and for being honest and open with me. i give you my class ring... for i have always wanted you to have it. you, and you alone. i'm not asking you to wear it, just to take it out once in a while and remember my love for you. your name is a song that will always play within my heart. i leave these things, my undying respect, and all my love to carmen... my reason.

this concludes my last will and testament.

donald wayne walton

14 july 1986

I'm proud of Don. Even at nineteen, he had considered the dangers of the Honduran mountains and decided not to go there with any unfinished business. As a born actor, he had also tried to script his final exit to make sure it would be uniquely Don. I would like to tell you that we followed his funeral instructions to the letter and all showed up in bright-colored clothes. But... since the funeral also included Tim and Bryan... and since Kay and I hardly knew where we were... much less how we were dressed... we had to wait a few years to fully appreciate Don's will.

These parts of Don's will have not been included as examples of how to write a will but as encouragement for you to take a few minutes to make sure that you will not die thinking of all the things you intended to say to people. In a world where there are a hundred ways to get killed every day, none of us should make assumptions about "the good death" at a "ripe old age." The steps required to communicate our final messages can be handled relatively quickly and simply and... once those steps have been taken... they can provide the same confident feeling you used to get when you went to school knowing that you had all your homework.

One of the simplest formulas for accomplishing this is to write a letter to your loved ones at the beginning of each calendar year. It doesn't have to happen on New Year's Day but try to have it written before the first week of the year ends. Then, update it every year. Don't worry about waxing poetic or creating memorable prose. Just say what you feel. Beyond the "I love you" remarks, there are lots of pieces of information that people need in order to take over the jobs you always did.

You can make the writing task even easier by putting most of the information in list form. Your list can range all the way from... "The insurance policies are in the top drawer of the fireproof file cabinet in the loose leaf notebook marked 'Insurance Policies'... each policy is in its own tabbed section and the first page of the notebook has a list of all the policies and their values and the contact information for each company." To... "When you are deciding how to invest the insurance proceeds, I think Doug would be an excellent person to consult with." To... "I'd really like that weird paper weight on my desk to be given to Mary Ellen." To... "One of my greatest memories of all is that day on Maui when we drove over to Hana."

Some of us will manage to avoid all the sudden death opportunities that lurk along our daily paths only to be ultimately done in by some terminal illness. When that is the case, we do at least have some opportunities to say our goodbyes, pass along important information, and perhaps plan our own funerals or memorial services. Laura's husband, Bill, lived three weeks and one day after his cancer was diagnosed but her memories of his final days are some of the most cherished of their life together. Though their relationship had always been a close one, the discussions that took place in those last days were particularly golden. An accomplished musician, Bill found satisfaction in planning his own memorial service and selecting the songs for those who would be present. As the days grew shorter, Bill orchestrated special times together with each of the children and grandchildren before he finally slipped in his own quiet dignity through death's door.

There's an old story about the last man off the *Titanic*. Whether it is true or not, it is a wonderful model for our final acts. Somehow, the hero of the story was not included when the life boats were loaded. Either by oversight or by choice, he remained on board. As the great ship sank slowly stern first into the ocean, the man walked uphill toward the bow. He stopped at various restaurants and bars along the way and helped himself to drinks, reasoning that he would need plenty of anti-freeze when he finally went into the icy waters. He continued his walk uphill toward the point of the ship tossing all the deck chairs over the rail as he went. He reached the front railing of the *Titanic* just as the great ship was about to disappear beneath the surface. He climbed over the railing and stepped off the ship onto a floating island of deck chairs, was soon picked up by one of the life boats, and never even got his hair wet.

I don't know enough about ocean liners or anti-freeze to say whether that story can be true but I do believe that it is a perfect description of the way each of us wants to encounter death... fortifying ourselves to the best of our knowledge... making all possible advance arrangements... and then stepping off into the waters without ever getting our hair wet.

Planning your death is one way to simplify the procedure and also have some fun. You should be prepared for people's strange looks and natural reluctance to talk about death... even to let you talk about your death. Your loved ones may even become concerned about your mental stability when in reality they should be applauding your mental maturity.

Choose a funeral director that you like and trust, talk over the options, and make your choices. Pay cash if you can and read the fine print carefully to make sure that what you want is paid for and that no additional charges can be added... no matter how many years may pass before you take delivery of the services. The exception to this advice is the person who is still moving from place to place a lot. But... once you have roots... pick out your casket or urn and your crypt or cemetery lot, save up your pennies, and pay for it all... in cash... in advance.

I hear more people talking about cremation these days than ever before. Jennifer decided to be cremated and asked her family members to scatter her ashes in the garden they all loved. Bill was cremated and Laura and the children lovingly scattered his ashes along the trails they had so often walked with him. Different people choose cremation for different reasons. Some are trying to save money. Some want to conserve space. Others want to avoid a grave site where friends and family members might grieve. It is something to discuss with those who are close to us. The place of mourning that I might wish to deny others could be exactly the sanctuary they need to work through the natural times of grief.

Cremation is one more example of the fact that what happens after we die is outside of our control. I know of one person who chose cremation under the assumption that it would save money for the family. When the bill came, it included the charge for the cremation along with a separate thousand dollar charge for "services of the director and staff" of the funeral home. The only "services" the surviving spouse could recall was opening the guest book. We do what we can... but we might as well prepare for the fact that loss of control is part of the deal.

I suggest that you avoid funeral insurance policies or time payments of funeral services. My friend, Lois, took out one of those policies in an effort to make her final arrangements easier on her children. But Lois died after paying only a few of the policy's monthly premiums. The insurance company was allowed by state law to refund the few premiums Lois had paid and then refuse to honor the contract. Pay cash if at all possible.

With your funeral arrangements made, sit down and write out some instructions about what you would like to happen at your funeral or memorial service. Take a lesson from Don and understand that your loved ones may be unwilling or unable to carry out your expressed wishes... but even so... they will have your description of your funeral to treasure. Every time I read through Don's will, I enjoy another rib-tickling visit with that curly-headed kid's unique sense of humor.

I have a few requests for my own funeral that I want to hereby pass along to whoever may be organizing the event. First of all... when they lay me out... please don't put me in a suit and tie. I never liked them while I was living and it just seems a little inappropriate to bury my shell in fancy duds. I would much prefer a blue Oxford dress shirt with a button-down collar and a pair of khaki slacks. Shoes are optional unless you suspect that a lot of folks are going to be opening the bottom half of the casket to look at my feet.

More important than the way *I* will be dressed is the attire of those who choose to attend the service. If it is possible to get the word out beforehand, I would like for everyone to honor me by showing up in their most comfortable outfit of the season. Whether it's winter or summer, dress for comfort. I am already enjoying the mental picture of my friends arriving in the clothes they like to put on when comfort is the only consideration. I trust there will be no neckties, no high heels, no tight waist bands. Wear your Bermudas or your bathrobe. Wear your sweat suit or your fishing jacket. Just be comfortable and know that I expect you to think of me and smile every time in the future when you put on those comfort rags.

I would like the memorial service to be one of rejoicing... conducted in full awareness of my confidence that I have moved forward into a better realm. I fully expect that... soon after leaving this body... I will be laughing and joking and getting reacquainted with Tim and Don and Bryan and a whole lot of others. And... if the dead are free to wander around earthly realms... I plan to be present at my funeral to go around and whisper sweet memories in the ears of the attendees.

Whoever speaks at the funeral should keep it short and light and stress the happiness of the moment for... even as you speak... happy reunions are taking place and even more are in store. There are a few songs that I would like everyone to sing. Simple songs with simple words for all to join in. Start with "There is a Balm in Gilead." Then, sing "There's a Sweet, Sweet Spirit in this Place." Then, "There was One Who was Willing." Then, "Up From the Grave He Arose." And close with "Let Us Break Bread Together."

At the cemetery, I would like for each person to be given a little party hat to wear during the graveside service. Then... just before the attendants start piling on the dirt... I would like people to file by one-by-one and drop their party hats into the grave. This should not only lighten the mood of the funeral but it should provide a real puzzle for the anthropologists who unearth this burial ground a couple of centuries down the road.

Instead of sending flowers, I'd prefer that people spend the cost of a flower arrangement to take someone out to dinner. Make the dinner guest someone you've been intending to get to know better but just haven't gotten around to yet. Or better still... take an old person to dinner... a person who doesn't get to go out to dinner very often... a person who has a lifetime of stored up wisdom and experience that nobody has been drawing on lately. Take them out... drink a quick toast to me... and then spend the evening exploring the treasury of your new friend's life experiences.

All the preceding ideas are subject to change since... if the situation allows... I would really prefer to have my funeral *before* I die. If it becomes obvious to me that some incurable illness is wearing me slowly down, I intend to set a date, rent a hall, send out invitations, and have my funeral while I can still be there. When George died, lots of his old friends made long trips to be present for his funeral. It was great to see everyone again. We had all known George and each other for years. In the midst of all the laughing and reminiscing, I found myself saying, "What a shame that George can't be here for all this. He would have loved this get-together more than anybody."

Even if you think it is "just too weird" to pick out your casket and pay for your funeral in advance, there are some very basic and essential legalities that are musts. Unless you intend to selfishly exit the scene and pile loads of guilt and responsibility on those you claim to love, you will make advance provision for a will, a living will, a durable power of attorney for healthcare, a regular power of attorney, and decisions about organ donation.

A will is the simplest thing you can do to be nice to those you leave behind. It doesn't have to be elaborate... but it should not be as brief as the famous will that said, "Being of sound mind, I spent it all!" You can get a lawyer to write your will for somewhere between $100 and $10,000... depending primarily on what kind of rent payments the lawyer is making. Or you can buy a piece of computer software for $50 or less, click in a few answers, and let your computer spit out your will. For years, I had one of those expensive lawyer wills but... since I had outlasted some of the people and organizations named in the old will... I decided to replace it with one of the new software versions. It took only a few minutes of typing in answers to simple questions to create a new will.

Organ donation is another advance decision you can tend to. In most states, it is as simple as signing your name to the form on the back of your driver's license. In other cases, you may have to fill out another simple form to assure that your wishes are carried out. If you are fearful that your body may be disfigured for the funeral if, for example, your eyes are removed, your funeral director can quickly assure you that measures are taken so that no one will be able to tell. The great tragedy with regard to organ donation is the huge number of people who would be quite willing for their organs to be reused and yet die without ever making the notation on the back of their licenses. It is not overly dramatic to say that... by signing your name... you may *save* several lives and improve the quality of several others. Don't let procrastination rob you of the chance to do that good thing. It is a decision that you can tend to now... even before you go on to the next paragraph. And... if the back of your drivers license doesn't handle organ donations... computer software can provide a clear, concise organ donation form that you can complete in less than a minute.

A living will is your chance to defend yourself in advance from those who might... by the reflex actions of their medical training... do things to your comatose body that you would not allow if you were still able to communicate for yourself. Since eighty percent of deaths occur in healthcare institutions, there is a high likelihood that your death will not be accidental or natural... but will result from a decision that one or more of your loved ones will be required to make. It will be a decision that they are unprepared for... that they are reluctant to make even if they think they know what's best... and that could haunt them for a long time afterward. You can spare them all that pain by filling out a living will. It simply states your wishes concerning the medical methods to be applied as you near the end of your life.

I talked to one couple whose living will desires were exactly opposite. He said, "If there's no chance of recovery, turn those machines off and let me go." She said emphatically, "Keep me going as long as it is possible!" Whatever your wish, your living will can make it clear to your loved ones. Again, computer software can make it a matter of minutes to tend to this important task... and it will even provide the form that is required in your particular state.

A couple of friends who have gone through the final decision making for their comatose parents tell me that a living will is not always enough. Medical experts can... in some cases... dispute, disregard, or postpone the desires expressed in a living will. They cannot however argue with a document called a Durable Power of Attorney for Healthcare. Specific rules vary from state to state but... just to make sure... I had my computer software whip up my Durable Power of Attorney for Healthcare. It was equally quick and easy and provides remarkable peace of mind to be no more than simple words on plain paper.

In discussion of Powers of Attorney for Healthcare, we should not forget to mention the importance of a "regular" Power of Attorney. This simple document not only smoothes the way of anyone trying to conduct business for you when you are flat on your back in the hospital, it can be of great help should you find yourself quite healthy, but stranded in a foreign country and needing a trusted person back home to tend to important matters for you.

All these documents are relatively quick and easy to create. The hard part is getting yourself started on the process. Like every other aspect of our deaths, the paperwork is easy to put off but a great reward to have behind us. Perhaps the most potent motivation to get busy and get things done is the awareness of all the problems and hassles you are sparing your loved ones by tending to as many things in advance as possible.

The last word in any chapter on planning your own death should be about *control*. Many of us are motivated to take care of things that relate to our deaths because we are controllers in life and feel driven to exercise any control possible during and after our deaths. The truth is that *death is about surrendering control*. We can make provisions but there are no guarantees. Unscrupulous or unfeeling people can circumvent any legal preparations we might have made. People are going to do what they are going to do when we are out of the picture.

Perhaps the most important step in planning for your own death is adjusting to the concept that you will no longer have control. Those of us who are compulsive controllers in life have an additional learning assignment as we plan our deaths. We need to create occasions in which we practice surrendering control. We will be shocked to discover that the world can continue turning even without our guidance... and... that people actually *like* us a lot more without our habitual drive to dominate. That's the way it works... things we do to get ready for dying almost always enhance the way we go about living.

13

WHEN YOU HEAR THAT I HAVE DIED

When you hear that I have died, you should know that the event did not sneak up on me. You should know that I have been expecting it all along. And... even while I was enjoying the daily life benefits of heightened death awareness... I maintained a curious fascination about *how* my death would finally occur. That fascination was a necessary part of moving beyond the defensive human tendency to think and speak only in terms of *generic* death. You should know that I put in a lot of hours thinking about death *in the first person* before I really came to grips with it... and... began gaining its daily life benefits.

When you hear that I have died, you should know that my life on this earth became more and more mature as I increasingly accepted the fact of my own death. If I had labored under the assumption that all I knew and valued on this earth would last forever, I would have labored in vain. If I had made myself dependent upon the continuation of this life, I would have been... as my father used to say... "leaning on a broken stick."

But... as I made death a natural part of my life... as I came to see death as a friend that would ultimately relieve me of a painful and inadequate body... I was better prepared to live my life to the full... putting more life in my years and worrying less about the years in my life... always ready to go... always keeping my unfinished business to a minimum... occasionally eating the desert first... and constantly looking forward to something better.

I was asked to lead the prayer at the memorial service for Jennifer. My words were honest and heart-felt. They express the eager anticipation with which I fully expect to leave this life:

Dear Father.

You do good work! We praise you for the things we learn daily about your wisdom and divine nature. Every experience we have tells us more about you and about the good things to come. We praise you this morning for life... and we praise you for death... and we praise you for the real life. We know how good life can be... and we know you've said the real life is going to be better... and we can't wait!

Father, we praise you for sunshine and for rainy Mondays and for the sunshine that comes again. We give you praise for mountaintops... and valleys... and for the land in between. We thank you for showing us that we have to go through valleys so we can remember them when we're on the mountaintops... so we can appreciate the mountaintops... and so we can speak to those who are stuck in the valley.

We thank you, Father, for Jennifer. We thank you for the Jennifer who was not in pain... who felt great. And... as we've said here today... we're all grateful for the health that Jennifer gave us when she was in pain. And we thank you for the Jennifer who is now... for the Jennifer who is having fun... who is in your arms looking up at your smile.

Father, we thank you most of all for your son... for the little we know and understand about his life on this earth... for the death that showed us that death could be conquered... and we thank you also for the life that he continues to live... a life in which he encourages us.

We thank you, Father, for life... and we pray that you will continue to work through Jennifer's great example. Help us to resist the temptation to confuse this life with the real life. Send your son back soon, Father, so we can end the rehearsal and get on with the show.

Every person who dies gives a priceless gift to those who stay behind. That gift is awareness of death and its manifold implications for our lives. Death awareness is about living. It brings the maturity we need to live our lives with wisdom and joy ... to stop cringing at the thought of eventual death... and start living with the daily enthusiasm of those who are packing for the big trip.

ACKNOWLEDGMENTS

My greatest satisfaction in life is to hear someone say that something I have written has helped them. Whenever people say nice things about my books, I feel like saying, "Thank you. I wish you could meet all the people who helped create the book you read."

Even before the first draft of this book, there were those whose life experiences, comments, and viewpoints suggested that there was a book waiting to be written. These include Bob, Jean, and Denise... Jim, Jan, and Jason... Bob, Carole, and Tasha... John, Joann, and Mark... Bud and Liz... Ron, Cameron, and Aaron... and Ross.

The first words of this book took form on the day Jennifer died. She was a unique human being and deserves major acknowledgment. I wish every reader who has come to know and appreciate Jennifer through this book could have the chance to know her equally impressive parents, Pat and Doris, and her sisters, Abigail, Joy, and Crystal.

Once the book was in manuscript form, there were many who took the time to read it and make suggestions that turned it into a much better book. I am grateful for the encouragement and suggestions of Rob and Karen, Pat and Doris, Jim and Marsy, Jerry and Peggy, Bud and Carole, Cecelia, Laura, Ross, Teresa, Eugene, and AP.

And the final four acknowledgments are those who made it all possible: Kay, the love of my life... and... Rick, Tim, and Don, the lives of our love.

Charlie Walton
August 1996

RESOURCES

Ahsan, M.M., *Muslim Festivals*, Rourke Enterprises, Inc., Vero Beach, Florida, 1987.

Bahree, Patricia, *Hinduism,* B.T. Batsford Limited, London, 1987.

Bayly, Joseph, *The Last Thing We Talk About,* David C. Cook Publishing Co., Elgin, Ill., 1973.

Bonhoeffer, Dietrich, *The Cost of Discipleship*, Collier Books, Macmillan Publishing Co., New York, 1949.

Burleigh, Michael, *Death and Deliverance*, Cambridge University Press, Cambridge, 1994.

Domnitz, Myer, *Judaism*, The Bookwright Press, New York, 1986.

Gomez, Carlos F., *Regulating Death,* The Free Press, New York, 1991.

Grollman, Earl A., *Straight Talk about Death for Teenagers*, Beacon Press, Boston, 1993.

Harwell, Amy, *Ready to Live, Prepared to Die,* Harold Shaw Publishers, Wheaton, Illinois, 1995.

Husain, Shahrukh, *Mecca*, Dillon Press, New York, 1993.

Hyde, Margaret O. and Lawrence E., *Meeting Death,* Walker and Co, New York, 1989.

Jones, Irene, *I'm Dying... and You Don't Know What to Say*, Vantage Press, New York, 1986.

Marcus, Norman J. and Arbeiter, Jean S., *Freedom from Chronic Pain*, Simon & Schuster, New York, 1994.

Martinson, Paul Varo (ed.), *Islam, An Introduction for Christians*, Augsburg, Minneapolis, 1994.

Morgan, Peggy, *Buddhism*, B.T. Batsford Limited, London, 1987.

Norwood, Robin, *Why Me? Why This? Why Now?* Carol Southern Books, New York, 1994.

Nuland, Sherwin B., *How We Die*, Alfred A. Knopf, New York, 1994.

Palmer, Greg, *Death, The Trip of a Lifetime,* Harper, San Francisco, 1993.

Kübler-Ross, Elisabeth, *Death, The Final Stage of Growth*, Prentice-Hall, Inc., Englewood Cliffs, NJ, 1986

Seeger, Elizabeth, *Eastern Religions*, Thomas Y. Crowell Company, New York, 1973.

Snelling, John, *Buddhism*, The Bookwright Press, New York, 1986.

Tames, Richard, *The Muslim World*, Silver Burdett Company, Morristown, N.J., 1986.

Westberg, Granger E., *Good Grief*, Fortress Press, Philadelphia, 1971.

Wiersbe, Warren W., *Why Us? When Bad Things Happen to God's People.* Fleming H. Revell Company, Old Tappan, New Jersey, 1984.

Wood, Angela, *Being A Jew*, B.T. Batsford Limited, London, 1987.

Packing for the Big Trip

Yancey, Philip, *Where Is God When It Hurts?* Zondervan, Grand Rapids, 1977.

Zaleski, Carol, *Otherworld Journeys*, Oxford University Press, New York, 1987.

INDEX

Packing for the Big Trip

ORDER FORM

Pathfinder Publishing of California
458 Dorothy Ave.
Ventura, CA 93003-1723
Telephone (805) 642-9278   FAX (805) 650-3656

Please send me the following books from Pathfinder Publishing:

_____ Copies of **Beyond Sympathy** @ $11.95	$ _____
_____ Copies of **I Can't Do What?** @ $14.95	$ _____
_____ Copies of **Injury** @ $8.95	$ _____
_____ Copies of **Living Creatively**	
With Chronic Illness @ $11.95	$ _____
_____ Copies of **Losers, Users & Parasites** @ $9.95	$ _____
_____ Copies of **Managing Your Health Care** @ $9.95	$ _____
_____ Copies of **Packing For The Big Trip** @ $9.95	$ _____
_____ Copies of **No Time For Goodbyes** @ $11.95	$ _____
_____ Copies of **Quest For Respect** @ $9.95	$ _____
_____ Copies of **Sexual Challenges** @ $11.95	$ _____
_____ Copies of **Surviving an Auto Accident** @ $8.95	$ _____
_____ Copies of **Violence in our Schools, Hospitals and**	
Public Places @ $22.95 Hard Cover	$ _____
@ $14.95 Soft Cover	$ _____
_____ Copies of **Violence in the Workplace** @ $22.95 Hard	$ _____
Violence in the Workplace @ $14.95 Soft	$ _____
_____ Copies of **When There Are No Words** @ $9.95	$ _____
Sub-Total	$ _____
Californians: Please add 7.25% tax.	$ _____
Shipping*	$ _____
Grand Total	$ _____

I understand that I may return the book for a full refund if not satisfied.
Name:_____

Address:_____
_____ZIP:_____
Credit Card _____ Card No. _____
*SHIPPING CHARGES U.S.
Books: Enclose $3.25 for the first book and .50c for each additional
book. UPS: Truck; $4.50 for first item, .50c for each additional. UPS
2nd Day Air: $10.75 for first item, $1.00 for each additional item.
Master and Visa Credit Cards orders are acceptable.

ABOUT THE AUTHOR

Since 1973, Charlie Walton has been a full-time wordmonger... providing scriptwriting, copywriting, and speechwriting services to business and educational clients.

Doing business as *The Wordmonger*, Charlie has developed a diverse customer clientele among church, telecommunication, education, training, and marketing executives.

Charlie's first nationally published book, *When There Are No Words,* described the events surrounding the sudden deaths of Tim and Don Walton and Don's best friend, Bryan. Charlie's unique way of describing the lessons learned through that experience has made the book a major consolation and encouragement to many readers when there were no words.